EXECUTIVE TOUGHNESS

THE MENTAL-TRAINING PROGRAM TO INCREASE YOUR LEADERSHIP PERFORMANCE

DR. JASON SELK

New York   Chicago   San Francisco   Lisbon   London   Madrid   Mexico City
Milan   New Delhi   San Juan   Seoul   Singapore   Sydney   Toronto

The *McGraw·Hill* Companies

1 2 3 4 5 6 7 8 9 10 11 12 13 14 15   QFR/QFR   1 9 8 7 6 5 4 3 2 1

ISBN   978-0-07-178678-2
MHID   0-07-178678-3

e-ISBN   978-0-07-178679-9
e-MHID   0-07-178679-1

Library of Congress Cataloging-in-Publication Data

Selk, Jason.
    Executive toughness / by Jason Selk.
       p.   cm.
    Includes bibliographical references and index.
    ISBN-13: 978-0-07-178678-2 (alk. paper)
    ISBN-10: 0-07-178678-3 (alk. paper)
    1. Executives—Psychology.   2. Executive ability.   3. Mental discipline.   4. Success in business.   I. Title.

    HD38.2.S45   2012
    658.4'09—dc23   2011027860

Interior design by THINK Book Works

McGraw-Hill books are available at special quantity discounts to use as premiums and sales promotions or for use in corporate training programs. To contact a representative, please e-mail us at bulksales@mcgraw-hill.com.

This book is printed on acid-free paper.

This book is dedicated to my beautiful wife and best friend, Mara, and to my three wonderful children, Jackson, Layla, and Genevieve. All of you inspire me to reach for greatness.

Contents

DEVELOPING EXECUTIVE TOUGHNESS CHARACTERISTIC 2

Focus: Improving Execution and Consistency

DEVELOPING EXECUTIVE TOUGHNESS CHARACTERISTIC 3

Optimism: Overcoming All Obstacles

Foreword

When it comes to mental toughness, I learned from the master. While attending college at UCLA, I played on three of Coach John Wooden's national championship basketball teams. He taught us perspective. Perspective to understand that a person's worth isn't decided by wins and losses but rather the effort they put into their preparation. Coach made it clear that it's a long journey, and out of adversity can come growth if you allow yourself to learn from it. Coach never talked about winning, but he knew more about it than anyone I have ever met. I only saw him lose a few times, but when it happened it was never the end of the world. A loss was an opportunity to get better and improve.

I wouldn't say that Coach Wooden talked about mental toughness as much as he embodied it for us as players. His most powerful teaching tool was that the expectations he set out for us were so clear they were divorced from outcome (which you didn't control) and all about the process (which you did). A lot of people break down and become overwhelmed by the potential for failure and they fall apart. Coach's whole philosophy was based around the idea that you don't control the outcome, but you *do* control your preparation, you *do* control execution, you *do* control teamwork, and you *do* control effort. He believed in "trust the process"; give me those things that I know you can give me and I will take whatever comes.

That perspective defines his mental toughness. He didn't have to talk about it because he believed it so deeply that he lived it and wholeheartedly role modeled it for us every single day.

Coach taught that mental toughness is the toughness that keeps your mind in control when your emotions are looking to take over. It is the toughness to focus on what you can control—effort and preparation—rather than thinking about what you don't have control over: results. It's a different sort of pressure. When the pressure is all about winning and losing, you have no control. Once he gave you all the control it turned pressure into opportunity . . . and a sense that because of our preparation and teamwork . . . it was an opportunity we looked toward with optimism.

We have tendency these days to believe the consequences of not winning are more dire and catastrophic than they really are. Let's be honest, athletes and businesspeople today are more focused on outcome than ever before. The problem isn't that they have clear goals surrounding results; the problem lies in the fact that they are so focused on those results that there is less and less emphasis on the process of what it takes to achieve those results. Coach knew that focusing on the process gave him the utmost control over the results.

One of the most important lessons I have learned from Coach Wooden is to "always finish." I knew deep in my core that if I could get to the finish line at UCLA, nothing, and I mean nothing, in my future would ever be able to get me to quit. "Always finish" is something I carry with me today; if I put my mind to something, I never stop short. I learned to never, ever give in, and I learned that every time you get to the end it makes it more likely that you will get to the end next time. Whether it is exercise, working through something difficult at work, or working through a personal issue—always finish.

It took mental toughness to finish writing my best-selling book *Be Quick—But Don't Hurry* while keeping balance with my motivational speaking schedule and prioritizing time for my family. I needed mental toughness in my work as president of CBS when many of my colleagues and predecessors were telling me the programs I was producing showed little promise and I should give up on them—programs like "Touched by an Angel," "Dr Quinn: Medicine Woman," "Walker, Texas Ranger," and "Rescue 911," many of which eventually went on to become some of the most successful shows in the history of CBS.

In my personal life, mental toughness was an asset when I sat in my doctor's office and he gave me the news that I had prostate cancer. The moment I heard the words "you have cancer" was one of the heaviest I have ever faced. I had to force my mind to focus on what I could control. Coach taught me not to waste time on "why me" or "how come"; spend your time on "where am I going to go" and "what next." It really took mental strength and fortitude not to get caught up in the emotion of it all and how the end result could go. But having the ability to stay focused on what I could control allowed me not only to work through it but also to enjoy my life while fighting through my treatment.

When you can move into the direction of mental toughness, when your mental side has won out, it allows you to essentially overcome the monster of results—the monster that masquerades as the fear of failure that you might not win. This is why Coach Wooden completely de-emphasized winning and losing, and it's why he emphasized effort and process. What drew me to Jason's perspective, first as a professional but ultimately as a friend, was that his approach to success embraced these same values. While completely getting rid of the pressure monster is unrealistic, I saw Jason's brand of toughness as a powerful tool for subduing the monster that empowered his clients not only to succeed in life more often but also to enjoy the success they created.

The executive toughness mental training program that Jason Selk has put together in this book is an effective way to train your mind for toughness and success. We live in a results-oriented world. Results are important. But if you can learn to control the "result emphasis" and highlight the "process focus," you become much more in control of producing the results you strive for. You may not be able to have the great John Wooden as your coach; however, *Executive Toughness* will certainly teach you to develop your mental toughness and take your game to the next level in a way that would have made Coach proud.

—Andy Hill

Preface

On March 25, 2010, the legendary UCLA basketball coach John Wooden inspired me to write this book.

The moment I walked into Coach Wooden's small but homey condo, I saw testaments to his greatness: book after book about leaders like Abraham Lincoln and Mother Teresa, volumes about basketball, photos of the coach's family and friends, and snapshots of the coach with various athletes, movie stars, and presidents. This collection captured the essence of his long, inspiring life—a life full not only of success but also of love and learning.

Standing in his home, I felt as if I had known him my whole life. You could say that I considered Coach Wooden to be my mentor—an idol, even—although I had never met him in person until that moment 39 years into my life.

My "relationship" with Coach Wooden started in my youth. A classic underachiever, as a kid I did just enough to make the grade or team. I was never willing to go the extra mile to achieve greatness—to be that student or player who excels by constantly pushing the boundaries of leadership performance and making those around him become better by being *the* positive role model of discipline and success. Then in the early 1990s when I was just about to complete my undergraduate psychology degree at the University of Missouri, Coach Wooden changed my approach to life. While completing a research paper, "The Ingredients of High-Level Athletic Performance," I became fixated

with Coach Wooden. His trademark "two sets of threes"—
"never lie, never cheat, never steal, and don't whine, don't
complain, don't make excuses"—certainly reinforced the
basics my own parents had taught me. What changed my
life, however, was Coach Wooden's emphasis on not making excuses. I learned from the coach the importance of
not blaming others for my shortcomings. Slowly but surely
I came to the realization that I would never achieve the
goals I had for myself without learning to give my best
effort, and to do so my excuse making needed to stop. His
definition of success continues to ground my personal and
professional life:

SUCCESS: Peace of mind, which is a direct result of
self-satisfaction in knowing you made the effort to
become the best you are capable of becoming.

I went on to read everything the coach had ever written. I poured over his teachings to identify exactly how
he transformed talented ballplayers into great men and
legendary teams. When I took his advice and became
accountable for my own life, I realized I had found not only
my own personal recipe for growth but also the basis for
the plan I would use to help others achieve their life goals
as well.

Remarkably, a few years into my career as a performance coach, I made friends with two of Coach Wooden's
favorite people, Tom Bartow and Andy Hill. Tom had
become close with Coach Wooden after Tom's uncle, Gene
Bartow, took over at UCLA for Coach Wooden. Andy
played for Coach Wooden and later went on to serve as
president of CBS. Together, Tom and Andy arranged for
me to meet one-on-one with the man himself. They told
me before my meeting that if the weather was nice, we
would go out, and if it rained, we would have Kentucky
Fried Chicken at the coach's condo. I prayed for rain.

Although the sun was shining, I found myself sitting on the couch in the legend's living room. Up close, I was surprised by coach's sense of humor. As he laughed and told jokes with Tom and Andy, I felt comforted by his warm smile. Even though Coach Wooden was well into his nineties and his physical health was deteriorating, his mind was still sharp as a tack. In fact, Coach Wooden had written more than 10 bestselling books *while in his nineties!* That's more than most bestselling authors write in their entire careers! At first I made small talk with the coach. I asked him a few questions about basketball and his opinion about the best coaches in the game today. I then found the courage to tell Coach Wooden how much I appreciated all that he had done for me. I told him my story, and then I thanked him for the positive impact he and his "no excuse" teachings had made on my life. Coach looked back at me with his soft blue eyes and responded with the utmost sincerity, "It means a lot to me to know that I have helped."

With tears in my eyes, I sat in awe of this great coach. His humanity overwhelmed me, and in an instant I knew that everything I read about Coach Wooden—his integrity, his ability to listen, his brilliance, and his caring—was all true. Coach Wooden in person surpassed his legend. In that moment I determined that I would keep striving to reach my own personal greatness. I was also inspired to write this book to help others reach and surpass their potential. And I knew I would do both the right way, the Wooden way, by identifying the fundamentals and then executing at the highest level possible.

John Wooden will go down as one of the greatest leaders of all time. Certainly, his form of leadership involved teaching and motivating others to follow his lead. Coach inspired his players to greatness, not just on the court, but off of it as well. Many give the coach credit for teaching them not only how to lead others but also how to lead *themselves*. Coach Wooden would say that leadership isn't just about leading or coaching others. It is first and foremost about leading yourself and truly *leading*—rather than following—your life. You begin to approach greatness when you know how you define your own version of success and dedicate yourself to performing at or above your potential on a consistent basis in service of those life goals. When you are indeed the best you can be, you deliver your leadership performance—a performance so good that it leads your life in the direction you want it to go. Because success is infectious, leading others will become the natural by-product of your personal actions and behaviors. Others will be drawn to you as I and countless others were drawn to learn from Coach Wooden.

I have had the great privilege of serving as a performance coach to some of the most successful athletes and businesspeople to walk the planet, and this book provides the proven, actionable path for delivering your leadership performance and achieving the greatness *you* desire. It builds off of Coach Wooden's philosophy that a focus on fundamentals drives success. The coach motivated his players to execute those fundamentals at a higher level than the competition. In doing so, he taught his players to *control greatness*. Not to seek greatness, or to emulate greatness, or even to achieve greatness. But instead to *control* greatness through attention to excellence in the basics.

I know, and have known for years, that Coach Wooden's philosophy delivers winning performances not only in sports but also in life. I've tested his theories in my own journey and with thousands of clients. By the time I opened my private practice, I had decided that my goal was to become the best performance coach in the world. I started by creating the concrete and comprehensive mental training plan that eventually became my first book, *10-Minute Toughness*. Attracted by its simplicity and effectiveness, Major League Baseball players flocked to it. Within a few years, I was coaching professional athletes from virtually every sport. Ultimately, I accepted a position with the

St. Louis Cardinals as their director of mental training, and in my first year working with the team, we won the World Series.

As my stock began to rise in the athletic world, more and more businesspeople reached out to me for assistance. Eventually I found myself providing not only executive coaching services to scores of individual Fortune 500 and 100 executives, but also consulting to their companies about talent and performance development. Since 2008, I have translated *10-Minute Toughness* into an executive toughness mental training program for these audiences. But it wasn't until my meeting with Coach Wooden that I decided to capture that program in a book for the business world.

The fundamentals presented in this book have worked for every one of my clients who has made the commitment to using them over the past 15 years. When I say *every* client, I don't mean most clients. I literally mean *every* client. If you, too, commit to using the 10 mental toughness fundamentals presented in this book, you will develop your leadership performance, achieve your win, and be well on your way to greatness.

Acknowledgments

Katherine Armstrong, you are the Michael Jordon of editing; thanks for helping me align the words on paper with the thoughts in my head. I would also like to give a shout out to my agent Kristina Holmes; thank you for your help with making this book a *huge* success. Thanks to Ron Martirano and all the great people at McGraw-Hill for believing in and supporting this project. Last but certainly not least, a special thank-you to Andy Hill, Coach John Wooden, Colonel Hirniak, Maxine Clark, Ben Newman, Steve at Wells Fargo, Nikki Hillin, Jim Steiner, Tom Bartow, Michael Staenberg, Justin Spring, John Ertz, and Dan Gable for allowing me to share your stories.

Introduction
Mental Toughness: Potentially the Difference Between Life and Death

t 8:00 A.M. on Friday, October 13, 1972, Nando Parrado and 44 of his rugby teammates left an Uruguayan Air Force base on a twin turboprop plane headed for a match in Santiago, Chile. Tragically, the squad would not make it to their destination. At 3:30 P.M. that afternoon, as the players threw a rugby ball around the cabin of the plane, the aircraft crashed into the Andes Mountains. The next morning, Nando and 26 of his teammates found themselves alive and struggling to accept the horrifying reality that would keep them on the mountain for the next 10 weeks.

Nando decided that he would do whatever was necessary to live. Through this conscious choice, he became *accountable* for the daily process required for survival. He worked diligently to prepare a makeshift shelter to help him and others brave the frigid temperatures and serve as a rudimentary hospital to nurse those who were injured and ill. With no food available in the frozen tundra and starvation approaching, Nando wrestled through the personal dilemma of using his perished teammates' flesh for sustenance. He refused to let his emotions overtake him, and he *focused* on using his mental capacity to avoid death.

After 17 days an avalanche hit, creating a certain tomb of snow for those who remained. Still, Nando refused to give up. After three days of digging, huddling for warmth, and fighting for their lives, Nando and 18 of his teammates found their way out from under the mountain of snow. While despair and grief gripped and defined many of his teammates, Nando forced himself to remain *optimistic*. Nando refused to accept failure even as imminent death stood directly in his path time and time again. He stayed focused on what it would take to survive, no matter the circumstance. On a daily basis, he worked to control his mind to emphasize and execute the solutions needed to overcome each and every obstacle.

After 62 grueling days on the mountain, Nando realized help wasn't coming and decided the only way to survive was to rescue himself. For 10 days he climbed in subzero temperatures across some of the highest and most unrelenting mountains in the world. Unbelievably, after 72 days, a physically weakened Nando emerged out of the mountain wilderness to safety and was able to direct rescuers to his 16 remaining teammates.

Nando's quest for survival obviously involved incredible amounts of the physical toughness that we might assume from an international rugby star. Yet the key to his survival and what set him apart from the others was his *mental* toughness. Take a look back at the story. You'll see the three key characteristics of executive toughness in italics: accountability (doing what *needs* to be done), focus (improving execution and consistency), and optimism (overcoming all obstacles). You'll find that these same three characteristics are used to divide the book you are now holding with the fundamentals detailed throughout as components of each. Mental toughness saved Nando's life, and I want you to realize that to be truly successful and fully satisfied with life, you will need to learn to take the same life-or-death approach to developing your mental toughness. Your quest for happiness depends on it. These same three characteristics will deliver the level of performance you need to achieve your personal win and approach greatness in your career and in your life.

Nando set his sights on survival. What are you aiming for? Are you aiming simply to survive your career? If you are constantly setting your sights as low as getting through the day and doing your job—the corporate equivalent of mere survival—are you really achieving the quality of life you want? Are you, like some of Nando's teammates, waiting to be saved by someone or something else? Most of us go through life waiting: waiting for the next big idea to strike us, waiting for the client to sign on the dotted line, waiting for the big promotion, waiting for the competition to run out of steam, waiting for the giant bonus, waiting for our spouse to change or our kids to grow out of a difficult phase. We wait patiently and politely, never realizing, as Nando did, the importance of deciding exactly what *we* need to do for ourselves and then pursuing those actions with relentless vigor.

The Characteristics of Mental Toughness

What you are about to read is intended to be a holy grail of developing mental toughness as it pertains to your high-level success as either an executive or as someone who aspires to become one. Although this book is specifically geared toward improving your achievement in business, the tools and principles it provides mirror the same methodology I use to enhance performance for anyone—from some of the world's finest athletes to the everyday individual trying to lose weight, stop smoking, or improve his or her personal relationships. The 10 mental toughness fundamentals presented in this book will work for you whether you are a high-level executive, entrepreneur, midlevel staffer, or independent contributor, because they translate Coach Wooden's simple, time-tested philosophy of identifying and training the correct fundamentals needed for success.

Much like athletic prowess, business success derives from a combination of physical and mental ability. The real key for improving consistency and performance in business is learning to control what goes on between your ears and then getting your body to follow through and take action. Business performance doesn't require you to fight through a 26-mile marathon, nor will you need to be able to hit a 96-mile-an-hour fastball. However, you will need to learn to strengthen your mind to a point that your body and your brain work together. Executive toughness comes from *mental toughness*.

MENTAL TOUGHNESS: The ability to focus on and execute solutions, especially in the face of adversity.

Executive Toughness shares practical stories of how real-life people have used this program to achieve high-level success. It is going to teach you not how to be busy but how to be *productive*. Presented as a step-by-step prescriptive manual, it will tell you exactly what to do to develop your own executive toughness and ability to perform so you can and will win more often at work and in life.

Ability is not God-given. Ability is learned, and therefore you can *learn* to perform to the best of your ability. Recent books like *The Talent Code* and *Talent Is Overrated* reinforce this finding. What is less clear is *how* you can develop your ability and learn to perform. *Executive Toughness* gives you that "how."

If you're like most professionals I've met, you want to achieve career success, but *not* at all costs. You don't want compromise, you simply want it all: a well-paying job in which you get to make a difference, a fulfilling personal life, great relationships, and health. You may even go as far as to add happiness and spiritual peace to the mix. In fact, *I* want it all, and after 15 years of developing my own mental toughness, I am well on my way to getting it all. While other personal development plans prioritize just one of these areas or use one part of your life as a means to achieve success in another, *Executive Toughness* imposes no such limitations. You begin by determining your top three priorities in life: you define *your win.* That means you do not have to choose. You can have it all, or at least the three most important parts of your all. So no matter if you define winning as making a million dollars, being recognized as a leader in your industry, becoming president of your company, fundamentally changing a market, making a difference in society, enjoying fulfilling personal relationships, being the best parent in the world, running a marathon, or simply being happy, these mental toughness fundamentals will work for you.

Mental toughness will require more than just stopping negative thoughts. It is imperative that you learn to fill your mind with thoughts representing your strengths. The mentally tough CEO doesn't magically have the strength to wake up before sunrise and make difficult decisions all day before returning home to his or her family full of positive energy. Throughout the day the CEO replaces negative thinking with statements like: "I can do anything when I put my mind to it," or "I am an intelligent and confident leader," and "I love my family, and I am present and full of energy when I am with them."

Thought control plays a vital role in mental toughness, and as we all know, it is much easier said than done. Success—however you define it for yourself, and you will do so in Chapters 1 and 2—is a fine balance between managing personal desire and external requirements. Executive toughness hangs in that balance; however, if you follow the comprehensive plan that is outlined in the next 10 chapters, the mental toughness that results will make you unstoppable.

Developing Accountability

Unfortunately, greatness rarely happens on accident. If you want to achieve excellence, you will have to act like you really want it. How? Quite simply: by dedicating time and energy into consistently doing what *needs* to be done. Most of us think we are invincible. Oftentimes, we extrapolate our sense of invincibility to convince ourselves that great things can happen without great effort. Chip and Dan Heath, authors of the bestselling books *Made to Stick* and *Switch*, capture our tendency to exaggerate our greatness with these statistics:

> Only 2 percent of high school seniors believe their leadership skills are below average. A full 25 percent of people believe they're in the top 1 percent in their ability to get along with others. Ninety-four percent of college professors report doing above average work. People think they are at lower risk than their peers for heart attacks, cancer, and even food-related illnesses such as salmonella.[1]

Many people clearly have an inflated view of themselves and their capabilities. Aspiring entrepreneurs want to make a million dollars a year and simply know their idea will deliver that result. But how many are willing to work with the purpose and passion required to generate such wealth? Thousands yearn to change the world, but they back down when the going gets tough. People want to live to be 100 years old even though they don't exercise, continue to eat as they please, or won't stop smoking. Everyone wants to be happy, healthy, and successful; however, very few have taken the time to identify precisely what they need to do to achieve those goals. This lack of connection between personal effort and personal outcomes promotes excuse making and justification for being incredibly average at work, and unhealthy and unhappy at home.

Many of us simply don't hold ourselves to a higher expectation; because of this, much of our work ethic has eroded and our ability and skill levels have suffered.

Accountability is the acknowledgment and assumption of responsibility for actions and outcomes. Simply put: doing what *needs* to be done on a daily basis. How far do you think Nando would have gotten if he had said things like, "This is not my fault," or "It just isn't fair that this is happening"? In choosing accountability, Nando said instead, "Success is up to me."

Being accountable in the business world is extremely difficult for two reasons. First, we allow our schedules to become overpacked. Trying to do too much creates the conditions for increased stress and pressure in our lives. Many of us regularly feel overwhelmed by all the things that seemingly need to get done—so overwhelmed, in fact, that we reach the point of feeling as though we are unable to do anything at all.

Cognitive dissonance (CD) is the second reason accountability eludes most people at home and work. CD is a self-protection mechanism that we humans use to justify our actions (or lack thereof). Our brains want our experience to line up with our beliefs, attitudes, and expectations; when there is a disconnect, or dissonance, we become so uncomfortable that we tend to change what we think to align with what we feel. Often, that change involves justifying our mistakes, blaming others, and denying responsibility. The increasing pressure we feel to get *everything* done creates a distinct self-preservation need to shield ourselves from feeling badly about our lack of personal competence. So we do what almost everyone else does when they underachieve: we make excuses. Excuses are the antithesis of accountability.

It is normal to make mistakes and come up short of expectations. The real trick is to learn to own mistakes and inadequacies and then move forward in a positive manner. You might be thinking, yeah right, who does that?

Accountable people, that's who! So let's revisit the definition of accountability from earlier:

ACCOUNTABILITY: The acknowledgment and assumption of responsibility for actions and outcomes.

I like the phrasing of "responsibility for actions and outcomes," but I prefer a definition that tells me *exactly* what to do to be accountable. That is why I prefer to work with this even shorter definition:

ACCOUNTABILITY: Doing what *needs* to be done.

Notice the emphasis? It highlights the idea that you cannot do everything all the time, nor will you *need* to. The most important part of being accountable is identifying and following through on those actions that produce the desired outcomes. Being accountable doesn't mean that you won't make mistakes. Quite the contrary. We are all going to make mistakes; the real question is, will you justify your behavior with excuses, or will you acknowledge your mistake and then step up to the plate by doing something about it? Accountability is ongoing and never-ending. If you make a promise to a client and then forget to follow through, will you give your client some excuse as to why you couldn't complete the task, or will you look your client dead in the eye and apologize, telling her there is no excuse and then going to work on completing the task? Accountability is finding a way to always do what needs to be done, regardless of how many attempts it may take for completion.

That's where the problem lies. On paper, being accountable makes so much sense and looks oh-so-easy, but we all know just how unbelievably difficult accountability is in real life. In the exact moment when accountability becomes important, even downright necessary for our growth and improvement, it also becomes the most evasive. Without accountability, we don't fully experience the need for growth. Apologizing to our clients when we don't deliver is painful and embarrassing, and we want to avoid those feelings. We would rather justify our behavior and let our cognitive dissonance protect us from feeling the discomfort and even pain of our lack of accountability.

I want you to learn to view the pain that comes from underperforming as the "gift of accountability." Allow the pain to serve as the motivation needed to work harder at becoming accountable to improvement. Without the pain and humiliation of coming up short, we have little impetus to change our current way of behaving. However, if every time you come up short with your kids, your spouse, your client, or your boss, you avoid making excuses and allow yourself to own the shortcoming and feel the pain of letting someone down, that pain can serve as motivation to improve in the future.

As you will see, being accountable is difficult. However, it is one of the most effective methods of improving your leadership status and ability. Chapters 3, 4, and 5 will introduce you to three mental toughness fundamentals that deliver unprecedented personal and professional accountability and growth. Even before we get there, I encourage you to get going by undertaking one of my favorite accountability exercises:

Accountability Exercise: Commit to full accountability for the next 24 hours. No matter what is on your schedule, make sure you follow through with every single thing you said you would do, and yes when you say to yourself or someone else that you will do something, you *need* to find a way to get it done. That is true accountability. Whether it be a promise you made your kids or spouse or something you said you would do for a client or coworker, find a way to get it done in its entirety. If you come up short, say the following word for word: "I'm sorry, there is no excuse, and I will work on making sure this never happens again." Practice saying those exact words now, before you need to use them. Today may mark the first time you have ever given a true apology for being unaccountable. Remember, an apology with an excuse or justification isn't a real apology. Others don't feel better when they hear your excuses, so stop giving them.

Increasing Focus

In the 2006 World Series, the Detroit Tigers were unfocused. Unfortunately for Detriot manager Jim Leyland and the fans, the team lacked consistency and underperformed on their potential. Leyland's Tigers, considered a lock before the Series began, rushed through routine fielding plays and struggled in the batter's box. They committed error after error (eight in total) and eventually lost to the St. Louis Cardinals in five games.

The Tigers felt an enormous sense of pressure to beat a Cardinals team that had entered the play-offs ready and focused on the right fundamentals for winning. Throughout the Series, Cardinals players kept their emotions under control and remained focused on baseball fundamentals by completing mental workouts. In fact, under my direction, the Cardinals players had been completing mental workouts daily throughout the season, and that investment in preparation paid off in the postseason. The mental workout is a five-step process that trains the mind for high-level focus resulting in improved execution and consistency.

So when people ask what made the most difference for the Cardinals in that 2006 season, I answer: "one mental workout per day keeps failure away." That's it. For athletes, that's all it takes to transform focus from a vapid pep talk into control and skill. In Chapters 6, 7, and 8, I'll teach you concrete and proven tools that culminate in your very own mental workout. The mental workout will take only 100 seconds of your time each day but will inevitably develop your focus, hence improving your execution and consistency, so that you will be poised for championship-level performance.

Before we jump into the details of how to develop focus, let's explore precisely how focus contributes to mental toughness. Most people agree that performance relies on focus. However, few people spend the time to identify exactly *what* they are supposed to focus on. Who takes the time to define focus, much less work on it? For the purposes of this book, let's use the following definition:

FOCUS: Focus involves selectively concentrating on one aspect of your environment while ignoring everything else.

Scientific research confirms that concentration is (1) a learned trait and (2) one that can be improved through proper training and effort.[2] Nando Parrado demonstrated tremendous focus by continually concentrating on nothing but the next step as he traversed some of most rugged mountains in the world. You can learn focus, too.

In the business world, focus allows you to execute at or above your potential on a regular basis. Think how great it would be to give your best presentation every time, make excellent sales calls consistently, or have every feedback session you give meet your objectives. By learning to improve your focus, you will greatly enhance your ability to keep your mind directed toward those control points that will most positively influence your audience, clients, and staff so that you generate results.

Let's take Janet as an example. An orthopedic surgeon, Janet used to struggle at times with concentration and precision in the operating room, especially in the late afternoon and evening. "I wouldn't even realize it, but I would be starting to slow down. My vision would at times blur, and I would literally have to step away to collect myself."

After identifying her top three focus points in her most common surgeries, she began completing mental workouts to improve her ability to concentrate longer. Almost immediately, Janet began to experience extended periods of mental acuity and improved focus. "The mental workout is just as it says: it's a workout that strengthens your mind. I do my mental work, and my mind is stronger. Now I am just so much more centered," she notes.

Developing performance focus is essential for execution, whether you are a physician, a musician, a technician, a politician—you get the point. Focus applies to every job if the person doing it wants to be great at what he or she does. We all know that losing focus can lead to simple mistakes that in the end can add up to devastating outcomes. First, you'll determine what tasks to focus on. Then you will improve your focus. Your mind will become a steel trap with the ability to be ready and focused on command.

Becoming Optimistic

Pain pierced the legs and lungs of 22-year-old Justin Hirniak as he competed against 50 other soldiers for the highly coveted admission into U.S. Army Ranger School, known as the toughest, most grueling school in the U.S. Army. A humbled and humiliated Justin had already washed out in his first attempt at Ranger School.

Now with three miles left in the seven-mile run culminating his second attempt at acceptance, Justin held his position in the middle of the pack knowing that he needed to finish in the top five. Over the past three months, Justin had realized that what had been missing on his first attempt was not proper conditioning or strength. It had been confidence. He hadn't believed without question that he was capable of living up to the honor of becoming a Ranger. He had therefore gone to work on his mental toughness. Even though his body was exhausted and shock waves of pain seared through his muscles, Justin knew he would finish among the leaders. "I just let my mind take over for my body, and I told myself I would finish in the top five. After a half mile of mentally battling back and forth, my mind cleared and a calm, confident state took over. I felt no fear or anxiety, and my pace continued. The pain and physical exertion went away, and my mental toughness peaked and rose to a new level. I finished the race third, went to Ranger School, and earned my Ranger tab."

Looking back at his success, he muses, "I believe that a key component is finding the right aim point of confidence. You convey this through mental toughness." Colonel Justin Hirniak eventually earned the post of Commander of Defense Contract Management with oversight responsibilities of more than 40,000 contractors in Iraq. Colonel Hirniak believes that every person needs to harness mental toughness: "It doesn't necessarily have to happen on the battlefield, playing field, or in the boardroom. It could happen anywhere—it's a mental state. The key is to identify it, make a trigger for it, and then harness it. Once found, mental toughness through confidence can be carried for the rest of life."

While Justin speaks of confidence, to my mind he is talking about optimism. Optimism and confidence go hand in hand:

CONFIDENCE: The belief in one's abilities.

OPTIMISM: Hopefulness and confidence about the future or successful outcome of something; a tendency to take a favorable or hopeful view.

Optimism causes you to believe in yourself and your potential to bring about a solution. In that way, optimism causes you to become confident. An incredibly important variable for performance, this firm belief in the successful outcome dramatically increases ultimate achievement. Some people think that optimism is a "soft" state of mind that is a part of your very nature. I disagree. Optimism isn't normal, but it can be learned, and that is exactly what Justin did in his mental training and what you will do in yours.

Of late, optimism is gaining momentum as quite possibly being more than performance-driving. It has even been called the "key to life."

Highly respected researchers like Dr. Martin Seligman, the University of Pennsylvania professor commonly known as the father of positive psychology, further contend that optimistic people are happier, healthier, and more successful than their pessimistic counterparts. For years, we have heard the adage "don't be negative," and yet, we also know optimism doesn't come easily or automatically. Telling a person not to be negative—especially during tough times—is usually wasted breath.

The "theory of dominant thought" offers one reason we get stuck in negative thinking cycles when times get rough. This theory suggests that we will attend to the dominant thought on our radar. For example, if I say to you, "Don't think about a pink elephant with blue running shoes," you will very likely think about a pink elephant even though I asked you not to. When you are caught in the middle of experiencing a negative situation (e.g., a sales call that ended poorly), it's only natural to remain focused on that negative event even though doing so isn't in your best interest.

Let's consider one other psychological concept along with dominant thought, expectancy theory: *that which you focus on, expands.* And unfortunately, human beings have the propensity to focus on problems, so our problems tend to expand. Your day may begin with an important presentation that goes unexpectedly wrong. Knowing that you have potentially lost a major account, you begin to worry. Then you carry that worry like a weight for the rest of your day. By letting your mind focus on the morning's problem, you project that poor performance onto three other sales pitches throughout the day. Not surprisingly, those go south as well. Now you *really* have something to worry about.

Mental toughness isn't for the faint of heart; realize that it will at times require the full-throttle intensity so displayed by individuals like Nando Parrado and Colonel Hirniak. Chapters 9 and 10 will give you a simple yet effective process for developing your own optimism so you can increase your mental toughness and overcome all obstacles to success just as they did. In doing so, you will see for yourself how mental toughness allows each of us to rise to the challenge when the pressure is on and *exceed* our potential in the process.

I encourage you to take your time as you move through this book. Stop to think and digest where needed. Allow yourself to become engaged with the exercises. Put energy into writing down your entries in the spaces provided. In doing so, you will begin your own miraculous journey toward unleashing the power and strength of your mind. As you begin, keep in mind that above all, executive toughness is relatively simple. It is not an elusive secret or a process that will take you hours a day to enact or years to perfect. By following the proven step-by-step plan you have in your hands, you will inevitably and undoubtedly begin winning the battle of the mind and increase your ability to overcome each and every challenge that lies in your path.

To the best of your ability, answer the following questions:

1. On a scale of 1 to 10, how accountable are you? How accountable will you need to be to accomplish your dreams?

1   2   3   4   5   6   7   8   9   10

2. On a scale of 1 to 10, how focused are you? How focused will you need to be to accomplish your dreams?

1   2   3   4   5   6   7   8   9   10

3. On a scale of 1 to 10, how optimistic are you? How optimistic will you need to be to accomplish your dreams?

1   2   3   4   5   6   7   8   9   (10)

Choose to Be Great

The three characteristics of executive toughness are accountability, focus, and optimism. You will develop your executive toughness through daily practice of these 10 mental toughness fundamentals:

- Define your win.
- Create your vision of self-image.
- Set product goals; emphasize process goals.
- Prioritize the priorities.
- Complete daily performance evaluations.
- Control your arousal state.
- Know your scripts.
- Prepare mentally every day.
- Develop a relentless solution focus.
- Adopt Gable discipline.

FOUNDATION OF MENTAL TOUGHNESS

What You Want and Who You Are

Define Your Win

Determine Your Purpose and Priorities

At an early age Maxine Clark, founder of Build-A-Bear Workshop, the world's largest producer and retailer of make-your-own stuffed animals, learned the importance of having purpose and doing what you love. Maxine's mother taught Maxine that "every person has the right to become all that they can be." Although Maxine's family was far from wealthy, they did meaningful things. Her mother cofounded a school for children with Down syndrome and took Maxine to political conventions. When Maxine was 12, her mother took her along on bus rides protesting segregation; they were both arrested. "When I was young, I was so curious and my mother gave me the opportunity to see all kinds of things. I didn't know exactly what I wanted to do with my life, but I knew I didn't want to be anonymous. I wanted to do something special. I know now that my purpose in life is to be my mother's daughter."

You don't need to spend much time with Maxine to realize she is living her purpose. She truly is a remarkable woman. Her presence does not rely on the fact that she has established herself as one of the top businesspeople in the modern era. Instead, it stems from her very substance. Quite simply, she cares: she cares about the world, she cares about education, she cares about people. Her passion and style are both refreshing and inspirational.

Maxine first made a name for herself at the May Department Stores, where colleagues thoroughly enjoyed working with her. Maxine's infectious creativity and innate ability to care propelled her to the top of the male-dominated retail industry. As president of Payless ShoeSource, Maxine experienced great success pushing this industry giant to achieve more than $2 billion in annual sales. "I knew growing up in the male world of business that you had to pretend to be someone you really weren't in your heart. That wasn't a bad thing. It was like putting yourself in a role that you wouldn't have played otherwise, and there is nothing wrong with that. But after a while I realized that my financial bank account was full, yet my psychic income was at empty. Ultimately I decided there was more to life"[1]

Maxine decided to move forward, but this time with purpose. "I had to remember who I was. I then determined what I wanted to do." After resigning from Payless in 1996, Maxine made the decision to follow her dream of doing something different and important. One year later, Maxine opened her first Build-A-Bear Workshop, a mall-based make-your-own-stuffed-animal experience that is enormously popular with children in the United States and in many other countries around the world. Ten years after its founding, Build-A-Bear Workshop recorded sales of $474 million and had garnered accolades for its deep, inclusive corporate culture in which every employee could make a difference.

The main transition point in Maxine's career came when she realized she wasn't on *her* path. She found the courage to decide what *she* wanted out of *her* life. In making this decision, she exhibited mental toughness fundamental #1: *define your win.*

DEFINE YOUR WIN: Know your purpose and priorities to solidify your ability to win in the important aspects of life.

You begin to achieve the success you want by determining your purpose and priorities. When you, like Maxine Clark, decide who you want to be and what you are going to stand for, you begin to rise above the masses in business who have no idea. You set the course for winning, quite simply, by defining what winning means to you.

A Scoreboard for Your Life

When you watch a baseball game, it is easy to know who is winning: you look at the scoreboard and it's right there in front of you to see. But how do you know if you are winning in life? The only true method of answering this question is to clearly define your win by delineating what is most important to you. This chapter will assist you in identifying your purpose and your priorities so you will always have a "scoreboard of life" that tells you if you are winning or not.

No one else can create that scoreboard for you; in doing so, they would be telling you what you want out of your life. Yet it seems that so many people—businesspeople in particular, for some reason—swallow a set definition of success hook, line, and sinker. The result is that they end up trying to live someone else's dream without connection. Whether you are currently successful or not, you can and will go further by making a conscious choice to create the life you want instead of simply letting the machine of your subconscious hum along on its own without accountability or direction.

So many individuals walk into my office believing they do not control their lives. The truth is that we are in complete control of our destiny, and the first step is to own this reality. The great thing about our existence is that we each get to choose who we are and how our lives turn out. In the book *Discover Your Destiny*, Patanjali is quoted:

> When you are inspired by some great purpose or some extraordinary project, all your thoughts break their bonds. Your mind transcends limitations. Your consciousness expands in every direction, and you will find yourself in a new, great, and wonderful world. Dormant forces, faculties, and talents become alive, and you discover yourself to be a greater person by far than you ever dreamed yourself to be.[2]

The flip side is that without such a life vision in the form of purpose and priorities, people become stagnant, sedentary, and worn out by the daily grind. A leading cause of depression, lack of a life vision is quite common. Oftentimes, individuals who have tried every medication in the book still end up walking into my office full of suffering. That suffering is their body's alarm system notifying them that they need to make some changes. The cure cannot be found in a pill bottle. The act of defining the win by creating a specific, actionable life vision-of-the-win can begin to produce relief almost immediately.

A Cy Young Award–winning major league pitcher told me this story about how not having purpose and priorities early in his career impacted his life: "When I was a kid, all this success came easy to me. I could do anything athletically better than other kids my age. I could surf before I was eight; skateboarding, basketball, you name it, I could do it. I didn't even have to work at it. Same thing with baseball. I have the ability to do things with my arm that others can't, and I really don't have to work that hard at it. My career just kind of happened without me really knowing it." But then the battery lost its charge: "The problem was," he continued, "that the money and success wore off pretty fast. I was absolutely lost because I didn't know where I was trying to go with my life."

Maxine's mother made sure she had opportunities to see the wide spectrum of life, thus giving Maxine ample experience to know what possibilities existed. Certainly, Maxine's early curiosity set the stage for her eventual determination of purpose. But in the end, both Maxine and the Cy Young winner had to summon up their own courage and dedicate their own time to design their own scoreboards for life by defining purpose and priorities. Likewise, your decision will take courage and time. So you begin your executive toughness journey by dedicating a few minutes to work on these basics.

Purpose

It doesn't matter if you are a CEO of a Fortune 100 company, a stay-at-home mom, a major league baseball player, a college student, or a gas station attendant: the truth is that until you identify your purpose in life, you will never reach your *full* potential, because you won't have defined for yourself what that potential could be.

To define your purpose, ask yourself: *What is my purpose in life? What is the overall main reason for my being?* Here are a few examples:

- A doctor I know has the purpose of serving others.
- A client of mine who is a corporate attorney has the purpose of achieving greatness.
- The CEO of a major pharmaceutical company strives to live each day with patience, contentment, and generosity.
- A gym owner's purpose is to experience love.
- A professional football player I work with believes his purpose is to make the world a better place every day.

There is no right or wrong answer when it comes to purpose. But it is important that you decide what your purpose is so you have a guiding light for how you live your life.

Unfortunately, most individuals have no idea what their purpose is. Many believe that identifying a purpose is one of life's biggest and most daunting undertakings. Sure, it's tough to know why you are here and what you are supposed to do. No one wants to answer the "What is my purpose?" question incorrectly, so most of us just don't answer it at all. Yet it all becomes easier when you realize that there is no right or wrong answer. It's your life, and you get to decide your purpose in it. I can't tell you to make it your life purpose to become a business icon while making the world a better place for children. Likewise, I can't tell you that this combination shouldn't be your life purpose. You must decide for yourself what you are passionate about, what you want to do, and how you want to make your mark.

Important decisions aren't supposed to be easy, but don't let that stop you from making them. Many people become overwhelmed with making big decisions such as identifying their purpose in life. The result: they don't make the decision, they end up lacking purpose and therefore underperforming, and they get stuck in a "holding pattern." Holding patterns are one of the most counterproductive and uncomfortable places to be.

When we fail to do anything through indecision, we open ourselves up to more problems. So here's my advice: in the face of decisions big or small, just pick a direction and then confirm or deny. As time passes, if the decision seems to have been for the best, confirm it in your mind and continue to take action. If the decision seems incorrect, then deny it and simply make another choice based on the new reality. Avoid holding patterns at all cost! Have purpose, and with each day and every correction, move toward it. Never look back, only forward.

Your purpose may change over time or as you put more thought into it. Figuring out your purpose in life will serve as your true north in many of your life's future decisions. Knowing what you are ultimately trying to accomplish will serve you well in many of the decisions you will need to make on your journey. It will provide you with great motivation and passion along the way. When it comes to decisions, *decide to always decide.*

> Trust yourself. Whether you are clear on it or not, take a moment right now and write down what you see as your purpose. Try to keep it short and concise enough that you will be able to remember and recite it quickly. You'll confirm or deny your purpose as time passes.
>
> **My purpose in life is:**
>
> help others, Leave a legacy (RT?)

Priorities

Priorities are the second important item to consider before you can fully define your win in life. While your purpose tells you *why* you are here, your priorities capture what you value. Ask yourself: *What is important to me?*

That's another really big question. As a multifaceted professional, you may come up with dozens of things that are important to you. I've learned from the channel capacity theory that most human beings can successfully manage only three priority items at a time, so let's hone this really big question to just the three most important aspects of your life. With that limited focus, you can be sure to achieve leadership performance in those three areas that are of utmost significance to you.

Begin thinking about how you would describe your top three priorities in life. Many of the individuals I work with list family, career, and relationship with self as the top three priorities. But remember, neither I nor anyone else can define your win, so those may not be yours.

Steve, a financial advisor with Wells Fargo, defined his purpose as "experiencing excellence and personal fulfillment daily." He went on to describe his top three priorities in life as:

1. Relationship with self
2. Relationship with family
3. Career

Steve expresses the specifics of his priorities in the following way:

The first most important thing in my life is my relationship with myself; I want to be honest, hardworking, healthy, fun-loving, giving, courageous, and connected to God.

My relationships with my wife and kids are also of great importance to me. I want to be present in their lives. I want to have a great relationship built on love and friendship with each of them.

Career is the third priority in my life. It is important to me to be successful. I would like to attain a great level of financial stability for my family by helping my clients have the financial stability they strive for as well.

Take a few moments now and decide what you *want to have* as the three most important priorities in your life. As with your purpose, you may confirm or deny these as you move forward.

My top three priorities in life are:

1. _Hlthy self_
2. _Good wife_
3. _Volunteer good_

Achieving Greatness

The first sentence in Jim Collins's seminal book *Good to Great* reads, "Good is the enemy of great."[3] Individuals and companies have a tendency to become satisfied with what is good, and the sense of satisfaction promotes an attitude of stagnation.[4] I once heard former coaching great Lou Holtz say that people are like trees: the second we stop growing, we start dying. Stagnation easily morphs into laziness, and once a person stops trying to grow and improve, he or she is nothing more than mediocre. I detest "the aggressive pursuit of being incredibly average" that so many in our society have bought into. Make it a point to become more than average, and decide today to complete the first step of becoming great . . . by defining your win.

Yes, it will take extra work on your part to identify your dream and put the energy into making it happen. Take the time to define your win, and you will dramatically increase your likelihood for personal and professional success. Follow this process, and you'll follow in the footsteps of industry greats like Maxine Clark, who win on their terms.

Choose to Be Great

Mental Toughness Fundamental #1: Define Your Win. *Know your purpose and priorities to solidify your ability to win in the important aspects of life.*

To the best of your ability complete the following three tasks:

1. Tell someone you trust your purpose in life.
2. Tell someone you trust your top three priorities in life and be sure to state them in the order of importance for you. (*The first most important priority in my life is . . . ,*

the second most important priority is . . . , and my third most important priority is . . .)

3. For the next three days, make it a point to look in the mirror one time each day and tell yourself your purpose and priorities in life.

Turn Up Your Thermostat

Heat Up Your Performance

Eleven days before his eighth birthday, Ben Newman lost his mother to amyloidosis, a rare muscle disease. Ben obviously missed his mom in hundreds of ways, some immediately obvious and some more subtle. For instance, without her supportive presence, Ben grew up with little to counter his innate perfectionist tendencies. Ben never lived up to his own expectations: no matter how good his grades were or how many points he scored on the basketball court, Ben never felt good enough. Recalling his childhood, Ben says, "It was tough, it was really tough losing my mother, and I was so hard on myself. I have to admit I was lost, but I guess my saving grace was that I knew I was lost and that something needed to change."

After receiving his undergraduate degree from Michigan State University, Ben felt overwhelmed by the decision of where to go next with his life. For a year he bounced around from job to job until finally deciding to take control. "One day I decided that my life wasn't going the way I wanted it to go. I sat down and made a decision, and that decision has literally transformed my life. I decided how the rest of my life was going to turn out, and it wasn't just a fleeting thought. I decided I was going to be a great husband and father and have a great career and that I would be happy with myself." Ben identified his purpose and priorities in life; then he created something I call a "vision of self-image," a 30-second mental video of the specifics of who you want to be and how you want your life to be in five years. In Ben's vision of self-image, he laid out the specifics of the personal and professional success he wanted to accomplish.

Every day Ben played his vision of self-image in his head. Slowly but surely, day by day, Ben's life began to take shape and he began accomplishing the things he set out to achieve. When things would get difficult for Ben, he would conjure up his vision of self-image and he would focus on it with great intentionality. "I work in a rejection-based business. So there were days when my clients wouldn't show up for meetings or they would just flat out tell me no. At those times I would take 30 seconds or so and mentally replay my vision of self-image, and it would give me the confidence I needed to make the next call."

Within eight years, Ben Newman became not only one of the most successful agents in the history of insurance giant Northwestern Mutual but also a nationally recognized speaker and bestselling author. Ben is happily married to his beautiful wife, Ami, and is now teaching his two children how to be good enough in their own eyes to experience true peace and satisfaction.

Unfortunately, Ben is more the exception than the rule. More often than not, hardships derail happiness and success. Ben's key to success lies in his commitment to mental toughness fundamental #2: create your vision of self-image.

CREATE YOUR VISION OF SELF-IMAGE: Take 30 seconds every day to visualize who you want to be and how you want life to turn out, and dramatically increase the likelihood of achieving your win.

Ben found a way to meld his life vision and his self-image together by constantly *envisioning* the specific details of what he wanted before he actually got there. Using the vision of self-image, you can achieve similar success and transform your concept of what you want in life into a concrete reality.

Where most people fall short with their vision is that they don't go into enough detail to make their vision a concrete and usable tool. Many individuals use their vision like a pep talk: they have some idea of where they are trying to go in life, and they periodically think about it. Don't get me wrong, I love a good pep talk; however, a pep talk usually only helps for the first minute of the game.

Just as a superficial vision that sits on a shelf won't drive a company's success, an ordinary, vague vision of how you want your life to turn out won't propel you to success. Instead, success like that achieved by Ben Newman comes from attention to detail in the vision that serves as a consistent reminder that you truly have what it takes to achieve greatness. By creating your vision in a methodical, detailed way, you elevate your vague vision to a true vision of self-image, and the likelihood of achieving the true success in life increases significantly. The vision of self-image is essentially like a vision with superpowers.

Self-Image, Self-Communication, and Performance

Before you can develop a transformative vision of self-image, you'll need to understand some basics about self-image.

SELF-IMAGE: Self-image is essentially how you view yourself—what strengths and weaknesses you believe you possess and what you believe you are capable of achieving.

Maxwell Maltz first identified the concept of self-image in his groundbreaking book *Psycho-Cybernetics*. I must admit that when I first read Dr. Maltz's research some 15 years ago, I was skeptical, to say the least. However, convincing research supports Dr. Maltz's work, and I have personally tested his theories with thousands of clients. I eventually found that the power Dr. Maltz ascribes to self-image is, if anything, understated.

He writes:

You will act like the sort of person you conceive yourself to be. More important, you literally cannot act otherwise, in spite of all your conscious efforts or willpower. This is why trying to achieve something difficult with teeth gritted is a losing battle. Willpower is not the answer. Self-image management is.[1]

So what the heck is "self-image management?" Self-image management starts with consistently sending the correct messages to yourself about *your self*. Continually focusing on experiencing the success you desire causes your own belief in your ability to grow. When you develop a true belief in yourself, you become capable and powerful. Creating a vision of self-image that matches how you want things to turn out will actually begin to develop and *cause* your desired results. But you can't "manage" that which you have not created. So that's why you have to begin by developing a vision of self-image. When you connect yourself to your vision by taking 30 seconds per day to replay it in your mind, you give yourself the passion and direction for high-level success.

Self-image is internally constructed: you decide how you view yourself. No one chooses for you, and you can't choose a self-image for anyone else. Self-communication (what you consistently say to yourself) is the strongest determinant of self-image, so it follows that *you* create *your* self-image by the way you talk to and think about yourself. The subconscious mind listens to what the conscious mind says and then develops the self-image. Unfortunately, much of our inner dialogue focuses on what we can't do rather than what we can do. When you spend your whole life telling yourself that you can't or won't amount to anything, you start to believe that message. As Henry Ford said famously, "Whether or not you think you can, you're right." If you tell yourself, "I can't do this work," then it's unlikely that your self-image will include a vision of yourself as the big boss. But it's equally true that if you begin telling yourself you can and will achieve your win, you greatly enhance your likelihood of success. If you say to yourself every day, "I have the confidence, intelligence, and work ethic to become CEO of this company," you'll be more likely to be able to envision yourself as CEO and ultimately become CEO.

Visualization is, in fact, the most powerful vehicle of self-communication. The trick is to transform your words into mental images. Imagining yourself as the CEO—actually seeing in your head the details of what you hope your life looks and feels like—is a much more powerful experience and leaves a more lasting impact than just using words to reinforce the direction you are hoping to move toward. I often tell my clients that visualization is like bringing a gun to a knife fight: your previously negative thoughts and self-talk won't stand a chance against the more powerful detailed visions of success you are about to create.

Self-Image as the Thermostat of Effort

I was presenting this very topic for the St. Louis Cardinals baseball team at spring training in 2006 when one of the players, known for his boisterous personality and aggressive work ethic, chimed in, "So you're teaching us to mind-f@*% ourselves?"

"A great question," I replied with a grin, imagining what would happen if someone in a corporate seminar used that vocabulary. "You are not mentally tricking yourself by developing your self-image." I went on to explain that self-image is a proven agent of behavior control. If you set your self-image high, you will experience an increase of internal motivation if you are not accomplishing goals at the self-image level you set for yourself. The internal motivation compels you to work harder or smarter until you begin achieving at the self-determined level of self-image. Over time, the self-image will regulate behaviors and outcomes to fall within the range of self-expectation. Essentially, the self-image governs how successful any individual becomes because it motivates and shapes work ethic and effort.

In this way, self-image is like a thermostat. If you set the thermostat at 72 degrees Fahrenheit and the room drops to 71 degrees, the thermostat then sends a message to the heater to get to work. Warm air rushes into the room, and the room warms up to 72 degrees. When the room reaches 73 degrees, the thermostat tells the heater to stop working. All day long, the thermostat governs the temperature in the room and won't allow the room temperature to rise or drop from the desired temperature for long. Human beings are the same way: we neither outperform nor underperform our self-image for very long. That's why it is so important to set your self-image gauge high enough to achieve your life goals. Set your self-image gauge too low, and by definition, you'll underachieve, because your mind won't call for the motivation to achieve more.

The self-image thermostat is why a substantial percentage of lottery winners file for bankruptcy within five years of winning. Lottery winners who were in financial straits before they won wind up back in the same boat five years later because even though their financial situation has dramatically changed, their self-image hasn't. If people see themselves as "not good with money," it doesn't matter how much money they have, they will find a way to lose or squander it. In other words, they have set their self-image thermostat low. Likewise, if you hold onto a *negative* vision of self-image, you will likely become that vision.

Therefore, a key to self-image management is to create a *positive* vision of self-image and set your thermostat high. I know that sounds like an obvious distinction, but it's an important one. Decide how you want to live and who you want to be, and then begin to align your thoughts with the self-image you hold. Your self-image thermostat will engage your work ethic to follow suit. Your vision of self-image will guide and direct actions and behaviors until the vision of self-image becomes reality.

Getting Specific: The 30-Second Vision of Self-Image

Without including the specifics of what is truly impor-tant in your life, you will likely fall flat in your attempts to achieve the greatness you desire. The same was true of Steve, the financial analyst from Chapter 1, who listed his relationship with self, relationship with family, and career as his life priorities. Until he created a vision of self-image including the very specific details emanating from his pur-pose and priorities, his life was riddled with discontent. After he went through the process of creating a vision of self-image, he looked back with appreciation: "Honestly, including self-image specifics in my vision has probably saved my life and my career."

Here's Steve's description of his 30-second mental video on his vision of self-image. Bear in mind that at the time he wrote this, Steve lived in St. Louis, and all of this, includ-ing the reference to California, was his image of what he *wanted* his life to be like in five years. As you read Steve's vision of self-image, notice how he symbolizes his purpose of "experiencing excellence and personal fulfillment daily" and his life priorities of self, family, and career.

My vision begins at work. I look around my new office and I enjoy what I see: lots of space, modern and classy furniture, several awards and certifications hanging on my "Wall of Fame," lots of windows, and a nice view. I also notice how organized and clean my office is; specifically, I look at my desk and see that everything is in place. I see the pictures of my wife and kids, I see a thank-you note from a client, and I also see my calendar with appointments filling the morning and early afternoon but with nothing after 3 P.M. Then I picture myself on the phone with a client—one of my A+ clients—and I see and feel myself confident, connecting, and listening. I offer good advice and then influence my client to make good, solid decisions with his funds. Then I picture myself after the call sitting alone in my office feeling true contentment with my career accomplishments. I look at the inscription on my favorite paperweight that reads "making money is easy," and I sit back in my desk chair and smile.

The next thing I focus on in my vision of self-image is pulling into the driveway of my new home, a house in San Diego, California. I get out of my car and walk up the ornate California sandstone walkway to the front door. As I notice the distinctive flowers that border the outside of the house, I relish the fact that I am home before dark. I open the front door and walk in, dropping my suit jacket on the banister.

As I stroll through my home, I look at the family area to the left and appreciate the fine details of inviting furniture and art, the flat-screen television, and the rich music playing through an integrated sound system. Toward the back of the house, I look to the right and see the hearth room and the kitchen with stainless steel, granite, and marble throughout. The back of the house is all glass with sliding doors that lead out to the patio and pool area.

I open the sliding glass doors and step onto the pool deck to join my family. The view is breathtaking and the ocean is right there. I can actually hear the waves crashing on the rocks below. My wife is sitting in a chaise, to the right. She smiles—not the "hey, honey, I'm glad you're home from working so hard for our family" smile, but a genuine smile of friendship—and this tells me we have remained close through the years. She is happy to see me. She is my best friend, and I let that joy sink in.

I look into the pool and see my son, who seems about 16. He is standing in the water smiling and talking to me about something that has recently happened in his life. He seems happy to see me, and I can feel the strong father-son relationship we have developed and maintained. Next, I look at my elder daughter, who is about 14 or so. The corners of her mouth turn up into a smile when she sees me, and she talks me through the highlights of her day. Then I pan to my youngest daughter who appears to be about 12. She is all personality and tries to get me to laugh with some funny comment about how I am dressed.

These coming-home moments tell me that I am confident I have prioritized my family and have been present enough to build real relationships with each of my children and my wife even though I am still extremely engaged in my work. I sit down next to my wife and see myself in the house's reflective glass. I notice that I have kept myself in good physical shape because I find the time to exercise daily. I see myself as the man I have always wanted to be: I am spiritual and confident, and I am happy and healthy. I like the man I have turned out to be. I am experiencing excellence in my career, and I am a great husband and father.

Steve's vision of self-image is detailed enough to feel real to him. He draws clear distinctions between his current and desired future lives—for instance, at the time he created this vision, Steve typically worked past dark.

He can see and hear the details of the life he hopes to create, and he can feel the pride and joy that goes along with becoming the man he hopes to be. Steve's vision is inspiring to him precisely because he has included the specifics of purpose and priorities, and he allows himself to feel how great the life in his vision *feels* to him.

Each time Steve "watches" his vision of self-image, it reminds him of how he wants his life to be five years in the future. It reminds him of *exactly* where he is trying to go with his career and the relationships with himself, his wife, and his kids. Playing the vision in his head reminds him of how important it all is to him, and because his vision is so real, it provides the passion and motivation to better prioritize what is most important to him.

Remember, you will not outperform or underperform your self-image for long. So don't sell yourself short in your mental video. Stretching your self-image to achieve more is an integral first step in the process of living out your dreams. Just as your self-image improves when you actually achieve great things and have the *real* experience of success, you can improve your self-image through the *imagined* experience of success. Creating and using your vision of self-image helps accomplish both the real experience and the imagined experience of success needed to grow and develop the self-image.

To create your vision of self-image, use the purpose and priorities you wrote in Chapter 1, and imagine who and how you want to be in five years.

Take a few moments now and write down the details of your 30-second mental video of your vision of self-image that emphasize your life purpose and your three priorities. Be certain to highlight your three life priorities by symbolizing in some way the success you hope to achieve in each of your priorities. Include the sights, sounds, and feelings associated with the life and identity you want.

30-second vision of self-image:

_____

_____

_____

_____

_____

_____

_____

_____

If you don't have the time right now to develop your vision of self-image, please make the time to do so in the next 24 hours. Creating your vision of self-image is probably the most important and the longest single exercise I will ask you to complete for this book. It will probably take you about 10 to 15 minutes to complete, but it will be well worth your time.

Once you have your 30-second vision of self-image, make a commitment to review it in your head daily. Research suggests the most effective time to imagine your vision of self-image is either right away in the morning or just before bed. Those are the two times when your mind is most clear and thus susceptible to the power of the new positive thought patterns. My suggestion is to ritualize a time that is convenient for you: the time when you complete your vision of self-image is not as important as the _regular_ commitment to actually doing it.

Now that you have outlined your vision of self-image, identify the time each day when you will "watch" your 30-second vision of self-image.

I will watch my vision of self-image video:

_____

Taking the 15 minutes now to create your vision of self-image and then 30 seconds each day to review it will bring your purpose and priorities to life and increase your motivation and ability to complete the necessary tasks to make success happen. This mental training exercise will improve your focus and performance so that your imaginary vision will become a true reality.

Choose to Be Great

Mental Toughness Fundamental #2: Create Your Vision of Self-Image. _Take 30 seconds every day to visualize who you want to be and how you want life to turn out to dramatically increase the likelihood of achieving your win._

To the best of your ability complete the following three tasks:

1. Set a reminder or alert in your calendar of exactly when you will complete your 30-second vision of self-image video daily.
2. Identify one person you think would benefit from developing a vision of self-image and help that person create his or her own.
3. Create a vision of self-image board (VSI Board) by attaching words, photos, and magazine clippings

symbolizing your purpose, priorities, and vision to a large piece of construction paper. Place your VSI Board somewhere you will see it on a regular basis to help remind you to complete your vision of self-image as well as to serve as a catalyst for staying on track with your dreams.

DEVELOPING EXECUTIVE TOUGHNESS CHARACTERISTIC 1

Accountability:
Doing What *Needs* to Be Done

The Process of Achievement

Goals That Really Work

Latricia's blue eyes light up when her two-year-old son races in the room and bulldozes into her legs. In fact, her whole world lights up every time she even talks about any of her children. Latricia, the director of supply chain management for an alternative energy company, is a loving mother, a great wife, and a very successful businesswoman. As one of her coworkers says, Latricia is the "kind of person that everyone at the company holiday party wants to talk to, and she has the exceptional ability to make those around her better."

At 5 feet 1 inch, with dark black hair and a glowing smile, 36-year-old Latricia doesn't look a day older than 21. Replete with fight and courage, she has used goals since she was a little girl growing up in Texas to help her develop personally and professionally in life. "My mom taught me the Prayer of Jabez. I would thank God for granting me the strength to have accomplished my goals even before I actually achieved them. I can remember praying and offering thanks for getting along with the girls at my school or doing well with my studies even before those things actually happened."

Latricia's mother and father were always there for her, and their home was full of love and support. Her high school track coach taught her to set goals throughout the season. "Coach was like a second father to me—to all of us actually. He was big on goals, really big on goals. He would have us set horizon goals at the beginning of the season, and then we would set next-step goals at every meet. He would tell us that fortitude meant keeping our mind strong by not thinking about anything other than achieving our goals." With this concept of fortitude top of mind, she set a goal to attend college, and she was successful enough to receive an athletic scholarship for running track and field. After the school lost its track-and-field program, Latricia exemplified fortitude once again: she transferred on an academic scholarship to Texas Christian University, where she earned her degree in business.

Recruiters fell over themselves to hire this driven, energetic young woman. Even though she had offers from all over the country, she accepted an offer in a management trainee program at a large local utility company so she could stay close to family. "I was 21 years old, I had my dream job, and I had just married my high school sweetheart. I had accomplished everything I had set my mind to. I would set a goal, stayed focused on it, and before long, it would happen. I was on top of the world."

Latricia grew into adulthood with a firm belief in the power of articulated goals. She exemplified, as you will see before the end of the chapter, the need for mental toughness fundamental #3: set product goals and emphasize process goals.

SET PRODUCT GOALS AND EMPHASIZE PROCESS GOALS: To achieve greatness, you must set end goals and place significant emphasis on what it takes to accomplish them.

We'll get to the precise meaning of the terms *product goal* and *process goal* shortly; what's important to understand now is *if you want to achieve greatness in life, you need to put significant emphasis into what it takes to get there.* This chapter will help you translate your purpose, priorities, and vision of self-image into specific, achievable goals and give you a proven process to reach even the most audacious life and career goals. By setting product goals and emphasizing process goals, you take the first step toward becoming accountable for your own success.

Goals have lately become so popular and overused that they are almost cliché. Regardless, you need goals in your life to be happy, be successful, and achieve your own win. The goal plan I am going to teach you differs from many because it focuses more on the journey than the end destination. Because of that difference, it will be much more effective than the goal-setting plans you're probably used to.

Each one of us has an innate desire and drive to accomplish certain things in life, and you simply can't divorce accomplishment from goal setting. David Kohl, professor emeritus at Virginia Tech University, has found that individuals who write down their goals will have nine times the success of those who don't put their goals on paper. Yet Dr. Kohl's research suggests that only 20 percent of our population has goals and less than 10 percent take the time to write their goals down.[1] So why is it that so few of us take the time to develop and make note of clear and concise goals? After researching this question for 10 years, I have come to the conclusion that the reason is, quite simply, we are *lazy.*

To escape from laziness and improve your performance, you absolutely must set goals to help prioritize what is most important and therefore is most worthy of your time and energy. Get used to the idea that you have to *work* for greatness; greatness does not magically happen by accident or without channeled effort. Goals will make you articulate *where* you are going and then act as the prioritization guideposts for your strategic plan to get there. You wouldn't run your business without goals, would you? Then why would you run your life without goals?

Obstacles to Effective Goal Setting

In my experience, people trip up in three ways when it comes to goal setting: *infrequency, under-accountability,* and the *paradox of the end goal.* To help people experience these goal-setting obstacles during a workshop, I rent a few Pop-A-Shot machines (those miniature basketball machines you see in arcades). Fun? Yes. Instructive? Definitely.

Infrequency

I begin by handing several miniature basketballs to each individual and telling them they can take only one shot, so they better make it a good one. After everyone is finished with their one shot, I ask them to go back to their seats while still holding their other balls. Then I ask, "How do you feel about taking only one shot?" Usually, participants feel completely unsatisfied.

Turning to goals every few months is as unsatisfying and as unlikely to result in high-level achievement as taking just one shot on the Pop-A-Shot. Most people in the athletic world set goals at the beginning of the season, and then they check back on them at the end of the year. Corporate America tends to use quarterly goals—quarterly earning reports for public companies, quarterly performance reviews, and so on. Looking at your goals once a year or even four times a year is not frequently enough. Ideally speaking, you need to think about and execute toward your goals on a daily basis. I strongly encourage you to use weekly goals, at the bare minimum, as anything less than once a week will significantly handicap your ability to achieve at your potential.

Under-Accountability

After the one-shot exercise, I put on some fun music, walk over to the Pop-A-Shot machine, and unplug it. I line everyone up, and let them shoot balls at the hoop for 60 seconds. It's a party: it's loud, balls are going everywhere, and people are laughing and having fun. After everyone has had an opportunity to shoot for 60 seconds, I ask, "Who won?" Confused, the participants look around at each other and then back at me, until finally someone retorts, "Nobody won, because we weren't keeping score."

Not keeping score is exactly the problem with many goal-setting approaches. Most individuals neglect to make their goals measurable and do not consistently evaluate a score, or progression, toward winning. Without keeping score, it's very difficult, if not impossible, to be accountable to just how well you are doing. The best way to keep score is to use numbers to track small steps of progress. In the plan outlined in this book, you will learn to make each goal measurable by attaching a number to each and every goal you set.

The Paradox of the End Goal

I call the third obstacle to effective goal setting the paradox of the end goal. When we emphasize the end result more than we pay attention to the means to achieve it, we come face to face with this paradox. For example, the baseball player standing at the plate thinking to himself, "I need to get a hit" is probably going to hear, "Strike three!" On the other hand, the player focused on the fundamentals of his performance (tracking the ball, executing a compact swing, following through) has a much greater likelihood of getting a hit.

Here's how I demonstrate this one with the Pop-A-Shot machine. I ask each of the participants to take three shots while saying to themselves, "I have to make this shot." Then I ask the participants to take three more shots while thinking to themselves, "Wrist on top of elbow, follow through." I then ask the question, "If you were the coach of a basketball team, would you tell your athletes to think about the end goal, *I have to make this shot*, or would you teach your players to think about what causes the shot to go in, *wrist on top of elbow and follow through?*" In almost all cases, participants agree the best method would be to focus on the process of what produces the end goal rather than the end goal itself.

Focusing only on the "shot," or the desired result, adds pressure and distracts the mind from the fundamentals of the process. Your mind can fully focus only on one thing at a time. If you are completely focused on the result, you cannot be paying attention to the actions you need to take to make it happen. Imagine if a sales agent in the middle of a client meeting begins thinking to herself, "I have to close this deal if I am going to meet my quota." She wouldn't have the mental bandwidth to focus on listening to the customer's needs, addressing his concerns, and selling the features of the most appropriate product.

Breaking It Down: Product and Process Goals

These obstacles point to a need for a goal plan that emphasizes daily process over end product. Moreover, research tells us that the emphasis on *process* goals not only produces a greater level of success but also is more enjoyable and satisfying. The fact is, you can't be truly happy, nor can you reach your potential, without doing so. A comprehensive plan therefore incorporates two very important types of goals: *product goals* and *process goals*.

PRODUCT GOALS: Product goals are result-oriented and are potentially attainable within the next 12 months.

PROCESS GOALS: Process goals focus on what it will take on a daily basis to achieve the product goals.

The distinction between product goals and process goals may remind you of outcome measures and driver measures from the balanced scorecard strategy implementation model used in so many organizations today. The concept is the same: break an end goal into smaller short-term goals so that when placed together, they logically lead to the achievement of the end goal.

Let's go back and pick up where we left off with Latricia. She earned her degree, landed a great job, and married her sweetheart. Up to this point, things seemed to come fairly easy for her. She was promoted to a management position in operations, had a baby, and then took a dream job with a wind turbine manufacturer. Unfortunately, within a few years, things took a turn for the worse, and it all began when her marriage started to fall apart. Applying her goal-setting process to her declining relationship, Latricia set a product goal to save her marriage. But this time, all of her fortitude didn't work, no matter how hard she tried. Failing to achieve her goals left her feeling depressed and without hope. "For the first time, I questioned if I really could accomplish everything I set my mind to. That was a terrible feeling."

Latricia found herself a divorced single parent with a demanding job. It was at that point Latricia realized she needed to adjust how she used goals. She decided that she could no longer just focus on the far-off end point of a product goal. Instead, to fight her way through the tough times, Latricia learned how to use process goals to break down a big goal into smaller chunks. She defined very clearly for herself all the things she needed to do daily to be both a great mother and businesswoman. She relished the sense of control she felt when she achieved each process goal, whether it was getting up at 4:30 A.M. to exercise, spending an hour with her son each day, or making one new supplier contact per day. "Being able to achieve these small, daily process goals is honestly the only reason I managed to land on my feet," she now recalls.

Latricia's experience learning about goals is pretty typical: we feel successful when we reach our first big goals in life, like getting good grades. It seems like a pretty easy equation: goal + work = success. But as we grow up, life becomes more complicated and our goals become multifaceted. Hard work and motivation alone no longer deliver success. We may feel overwhelmed, maybe even depressed, like Latricia, when what used to work doesn't work anymore. We realize somewhere along the way that we need a *strategy* for achieving the big goals—a strategy that restores our sense of control, delivers feelings of success, and tells us what to do each day.

I choose this particular story about Latricia because many of the business professionals I work with are fairly good at using product goals in their careers and personal lives. However, they are nowhere near as proficient at using process goals in either. Learning to use product and process goals in all of your priority areas of life, both personal and professional, creates a powerful, synergistic effect. Improvement in one area creates confidence in another, and soon you are able to "win" your whole package rather than jeopardizing success in one area of your life to feed another. A career without a fulfilling personal life wouldn't be my definition of a win, and it doesn't have to be yours if you use this goal plan across all of your priorities.

Product Goals

You will start by translating the priorities you defined in Chapter 1 and your vision of self-image from Chapter 2 into three specific, measurable goals. At work, you may have been challenged to come up with "BHAGs: big hairy audacious goals," as suggested by leadership gurus Jim Collins and Jerry Porras. They say that a "true BHAG is clear and compelling, serves as unifying focal point of effort, and acts as a clear catalyst for team spirit. It has a clear finish line, so the organization can know when it has achieved the goal; people like to shoot for finish lines."[2]

Your product goals are similar to your personal BHAGs. But instead of unifying a group of people and energizing a team, they unify your efforts and encourage your motivation. Just as you would include a measurable finish line in business objectives, you should put quantifiable data points and time frames in each of your products' goals—even the ones related to your personal life—so you can keep score and be accountable to yourself.

Examples of career product goals:

- Make $1,000,000 in the upcoming year.
- Be the top salesperson in the division by the fiscal year end.
- Lead my team to sell 1 million units within 12 months.
- Manage my department to achieve 100 percent customer satisfaction within six months.
- Publish an article in a peer-reviewed journal by next January 15.
- Earn a promotion to vice president within a year.

Examples of personal product goals could be:

- Lose 20 pounds in 12 months.
- Run the Napa Marathon in less than four hours this year.
- Be the best parent I can be (on a 10-point scale, go from a 6 to an 8) by year end.
- Be the best spouse I can be (on a 10-point scale, go from a 7 to a 9) by my wife's next birthday.

Note how every product goal is measurable, and it needs to have the potential achievement date within a year. As you get to the other less definable priorities, like relationships, use a 10-point scale to create a unit of measure for these more intangible goals. Evaluate your current position on that scale, and then set the goal for improvement up the scale.

Process Goals

Product goals are all great end points, and writing them down is an important first step. But the truth is that setting product goals is the easy part, and that is precisely where most individuals stop short. The real key is to develop two or three process goals for each of your product goals. Remember, the process goals are the "what it takes on a daily basis" to achieve the product goals. Sometimes, a process goal may happen less frequently than every day, but it still needs to occur on a regular basis to drive the achievement of the product goal.

To demonstrate how process goals work, let's see how Steve approached breaking down his career product goal of making $500,000 in the next year. He came up with the following three process goals, which he calls 20-3-90:

- **Process Goal 1:** 20 dials per day (10 phone calls to existing clients and 10 to new B+ or better prospects)
- **Process Goal 2:** 3 face-to-face client meetings per day (B+ or better prospects or existing clients)
- **Process Goal 3:** 90 minutes per day preparing or organizing (market research, identifying B+ or better clients, keeping an eye on his competition, planning his call list), completing his mental workout (to be explained in upcoming chapters), and evaluating his performance (also covered in upcoming chapters).

Steve also set a personal product goal of improving his relationships with family. At the start, he gave himself a 6 on a 10-point scale, and he set a goal of attaining an 8 within 12 months. Steve identified the following three process goals to achieve that growth:

- **Process Goal 1:** Be home by 5:30 at least five nights per week.
- **Process Goal 2:** Spend 15 minutes quality time with each child nightly (phones turned off and no TV).
- **Process Goal 3:** Spend 30 minutes quality time with my wife nightly (phones turned off and no TV).

To fill out the picture, here's the detail for his remaining priority:

Product Goal: Improve Relationships with Self from a 6 to an 8
- **Process Goal 1:** Attend, at minimum, one church service per week.
- **Process Goal 2:** 30 minutes cardio exercise at least four times per week, limit fat gram intake during the week to 50 grams daily, and get seven hours sleep minimum of five nights weekly.
- **Process Goal 3:** Read 15 minutes per day.

Let's break some of the other examples of product goals into process goals:

PRODUCT GOAL	POSSIBLE PROCESS GOALS
Be the top sales-person in the division next year.	Make 10 phone calls each day to existing clients.
	Spend 60 minutes per day identifying and developing referred leads list.
	Make 10 phone calls per day to new referred lead clients.

(continued)

PRODUCT GOAL	POSSIBLE PROCESS GOALS
Lead my team to sell 1 million units in 12 months.	Identify one new "contact of influence" (connections to at least three chains) per day.
	Conduct daily 15-minute team huddles to replace all team meetings.
	Emphasize and track the wins by updating "team wins" board one time each day.
Manage my department to achieve 100 percent customer satisfaction.	On 100 percent of customer interaction, ask if there is anything else I can do for them.
	Each day, resolve five outstanding customer complaints.
	Each day, ask one customer service representative what we could do to improve customer satisfaction.
Lose 20 pounds in 12 months.	Limit fat intake to 50 grams per day.
	Cardio exercise at least 30 minutes per day (minimum three days per week).
	One time per day, write down everything I ate that day in a food journal.
Be the best parent I can be (on a 10-point scale, go from a 6 to an 8).	Once a month, have one-on-one date with each of the kids (by the tenth of each month).
	Complete start-of-day mental workouts five days per week to focus on arriving home nightly with positive energy (on the 10-point scale, 7 or better).
	Spend five minutes nightly alone with each child going over highs and lows of the day.

At this point you might be thinking, "There is no way I can add even one more thing into my already overloaded schedule!" Although mental toughness may feel like an add-on right now, I assure you that using product and process goals will immediately help you move from being "busy" to being *productive*.

Not having a minute of time to even catch your breath throughout the day is no way to live. You cannot possibly do daily everything that you convince yourself needs to be done. To feel good about yourself, you need to do fewer things, better. You do that by identifying what is truly important in life. In so doing, you prioritize only those goals that produce hard and fast results. You won't be choosing goals for every component of your personal and professional life. Instead, you pick three big goals (one for each of your life priorities) and break each one down into three daily goals. You spend your energy being productive on those process tasks rather than on being busy and pulled in all directions. And because of the way our minds work, that feeling grows into an even deeper reality that propels you closer and closer to your win every single day.

Defining the *Correct* Fundamentals to Include in Your Process Goals

Clearly, process goals will lead to the achievement of a product goal only if they are indeed the right fundamentals for that goal. Believe it or not, many individuals spend the majority of their day working on developing the wrong fundamentals. Let's use an exercise to see just how much effort you are putting into the fundamentals necessary for you to achieve greatness in your career.

You'll begin by listing all the tasks you complete at work over the course of a week. To understand what I mean by a task, take a look at some of the 27 daily and weekly tasks that Steve listed:

- Track market activity by watching CNBC and other financial TV shows.
- Oversee or coach junior financial advisors.
- Attend meetings about market activity.
- Return voice mails.
- Return e-mails.

- Organize desk.
- Write proposals for new business.
- Prospect for new business.
- Identify referred lead prospects.
- Call current clients.
- Meet with clients.
- Fill orders.
- Create files for clients.
- Undertake competitive market research.

Think about the last day you worked. Start at the beginning of your day, and remember all the things you put time into. Go through a few days in your mind to develop your comprehensive weekly list. Take a few minutes, and fill in *the first column* of the work tasks exercise now.

Work Tasks Exercise

	WORK TASKS COMPLETED WEEKLY	% AVERAGE TIME SPENT WEEKLY	IMPORTANCE RANK
1.	_____	_____	_____
2.	_____	_____	_____
3.	_____	_____	_____
4.	_____	_____	_____
5.	_____	_____	_____
6.	_____	_____	_____
7.	_____	_____	_____
8.	_____	_____	_____

9. _____ _____ _____

10. _____ _____ _____

11. _____ _____ _____

12. _____ _____ _____

13. _____ _____ _____

14. _____ _____ _____

15. _____ _____ _____

16. _____ _____ _____

17. _____ _____ _____

18. _____ _____ _____

19. _____ _____ _____

20. _____ _____ _____

21. _____ _____ _____

22. _____ _____ _____

23. _____ _____ _____

24. _____ _____ _____

25. _____ _____ _____

Now estimate the percentage of time you put into each task over the course of a week, and put the number in the second column. The numbers in this column should add up to 100.

The three tasks Steve was putting the greatest amount of time weekly into were:

Work Tasks Exercise

WORK TASKS COMPLETED WEEKLY	% AVERAGE TIME SPENT WEEKLY	IMPORTANCE RANK
Attend meetings about market activity.	20	_____
Return e-mails.	20	_____
Track market activity.	15	_____

Of Steve's 20 or so other tasks, no single task took more than 15 percent of his time.

The next assignment involves ranking the importance from most important task to least important task in terms of its direct impact on your professional success. To do this part of the exercise, you have to first understand how you define success in your career. Whether you define your career success as how much money you make, how much positive impact you make on the world, or anything in between the two, keep your definition in mind while you complete this exercise.

Next, in the third column, rank each task on your list from the most important to least important.

As a point of reference, here are the most important lines of Steve's work sheet at this point:

Work Tasks Exercise

WORK TASKS COMPLETED WEEKLY	% AVERAGE TIME SPENT WEEKLY	IMPORTANCE RANK
Attend meetings about market activity.	20	16
Return e-mails.	20	13
Track market activity.	15	9
Client contact.	12	1
Prospect new business.	8	2
Identify referred lead prospects.	5	3

Note that the three most important tasks for his professional success (which Steve defines as making more money) had been granted a combined total of 25 percent of his time.

The preceding exercise typically illustrates that individuals will spend a majority of their week on only three tasks; in Steve's case, he was spending 55 percent of his time attending meetings, returning e-mails, and tracking market activity. The "power of three" phenomena shows up often because of channel capacity, an idea introduced in Chapter 1: our mind can usually maintain focus on only a certain number of concepts at a time, and that magic number happens to be three.

How many of your top three most important tasks are also those tasks you spend the most time on? On average, the majority of people spend around 33 percent of their time on their three most important tasks. If you are doing better than that, congratulations! If not, what do you think Coach Wooden would say about spending only 33 percent of practice time on the most important fundamentals? Most individuals prioritize their time on tasks that are not the most crucial for professional or personal success. But the individuals who experience the greatest levels of success are those who have identified the tasks—the process goals—that are most important, and they have prioritized those tasks by spending the greatest amount of time daily completing them.

Feel free to go through the same exercise for all three of your life priorities, even the ones outside of work. It's a great way to figure out exactly what you are doing with your time.

Three Product Goals, Three Process Goals

By coming up with only three product goals to nurture over the coming year and having three process goals for each product goal to emphasize, you immediately overcome the paradox of the end goal. Chapter 4 will teach you a daily evaluation system that will allow you to overcome infrequency and under-accountability as obstacles to effective goal setting.

It's important as you go through your product and process goals to list them in order of importance to you. For example, if you listed your relationship with family as one of your product goals and you feel it is the most important priority in your life, list that as your priority 1 product goal. It should come as no surprise, however, that if you are prioritizing your work over your family, they will know it. Then they will, in turn, need to deprioritize their relationship with you to protect themselves from feeling unimportant. For this reason, it's important to list all three of your product goals in order of importance. Remember that you are likely to be nine times more successful if you actually write down your goals, so it's really important to grab a pen and actually put it to paper instead of just thinking about them.

Set one product and three process goals for each of your three priorities in life. Use the 10-point scale for those less measurable goals, and remember to include a current assessment of where you are on the 10-point scale as well as a 1–10 goal of where you hope to be. Every product and process goal must have a number attached to it so that it can actually be measured. In addition, try to make all process goals daily activities rather than listing them as weekly, monthly, or yearly. This will help keep you from back-loading your week with your process goals to a point where it becomes unrealistic to accomplish them.

Priority 1 Product Goal: _____

- Process Goal: _____

- Process Goal: _____

- Process Goal: _____

Priority 2 Product Goal: _____

- Process Goal: _____

- Process Goal: _____

- Process Goal: _____

Priority 3 Product Goal: _____

- Process Goal: _____

- Process Goal: _____

- Process Goal: _____

Take a moment to review each of your product goals and ensure they are measurable: double-check that every product and process goal has a number attached to it and that each process goal is listed as a daily activity when possible. If not, please take the time to do so now to increase your ability to hold yourself accountable for their achievement.

While process goals may be a challenging concept for you, they will help you focus on the cause behind the result and make life a more enjoyable experience as well as give you complete control of your life. Unfortunately, in our society and in traditional corporate models, the achievement of end, or product, goals stands as the measurement of worth. The amount of money you make, the type of car you drive, or the annual sales or market capitalization of your company carry more weight than how well you prepare for a meeting, how much effort you put into your work, the intrinsic quality of your products, or the strength of your leadership team. When you step out of the ordinary path and redefine your success as the accomplishment of process goals (an effort-based definition of success), you will have a much greater likelihood of achieving more and more of your product goal results. When you train your mind to become more process oriented, you will perform better under pressure and you gain control over product goal accomplishment.

Choose to Be Great

Mental Toughness Fundamental #3: Set Product Goals and Emphasize Process Goals. *If you want to achieve greatness in life, you need to put significant emphasis into what it takes to get there.*

To the best of your ability, complete the following three tasks:

1. Tell one person you trust all three of your product goals along with their subsequent process goals.
2. Look at yourself in the mirror, and state all three of your product goals along with their subsequent process goals, but this time state your goals as though they have already been achieved (e.g., this past year I improved as a husband from a 7 to a 9, and I did it by being home by 5:30 at least six nights per week and spending at least 30 minutes quality time per night with my spouse).
3. Tell another person you trust all three of your product goals along with their subsequent process goals. Again, state your goals as though they have already been achieved.

CHAPTER 4

Prioritizing the Priorities

Schedule It or Forget It

Arm in; shoulders up; step, step, slide; cha, cha, cha. Jim Steiner entered day two of the dance competition knowing that he could do better: "I was tight on the first day. I knew I was capable of more. I knew I was prepared and as soon as I got my mind right, I found my groove." After two days of moving and grooving, Steiner awed the crowd and judges into voting him among the "top 20 newcomers" out of more than 200 of the nation's toughest competitors.

Six months earlier, Jim had won his country club's highly competitive match play golf championship. With the pressure mounting, Jim relied heavily on his composure and ability: "It wasn't like I made any single outstanding shot to win it. I just played solid golf throughout and didn't make mistakes. All the practice I put in had prepared me really well. I went out and played, quite simply, like I had been practicing."

Jim Steiner isn't a professional dancer, nor is he a golf pro. He's just very good at prioritizing his priorities.

Thirty-five years ago, Jim Steiner started working as a sports agent for so little money it wasn't worth counting. For years, Jim stayed on track by prioritizing the most important aspects of the job: the fundamentals of building relationships and preparing each day to be one step ahead of the competition. In looking back over his career, Jim emphasizes that a sports agency is a personal service business. His advice: "Don't chase the money. Money won't make you successful. Chase success; that will make you successful."

Jim's approach paid off. He is one of four football agents for industry-leader CAA Sports, and Jim is considered one of the top football sports agents in the world. If you're watching an NFL game, chances are you're watching one of CAA Sports' clients. In fact, you're probably watching a bunch of CAA's clients: their client list reads like the who's who in professional football and includes Hall of Famer Jerry Rice, the Manning brothers, Adrian Peterson, and Sam Bradford, to name a few.

Despite this career success, a few years earlier when Jim was beginning to prepare for the future, he realized he needed to reprioritize what was important in his life: "For the previous 20 years, all I had really thought about was my career and my family. My kids were grown and doing great, and my career probably couldn't have gone any better. I needed to figure out what the next leg of my journey was going to be."

Jim prioritized staying connected to his wife and kids while searching for his next passion: "If you had told me 15 years ago that I would be a competitive dancer and playing golf as well as I am now, I would have said you were nuts."

While most of us merely think about doing what's needed to achieve a high level of happiness and success, Jim Steiner prioritizes and takes action. Once Jim decided that he wanted to become a competitive dancer and better golfer, he set up the following process goals:

- Attend one dance lesson per week.
- Practice or play golf at least three times per week.

Jim prioritized his new process goals in the same way he had gone about capturing career success: he translated the fundamentals into process goals and locked in time on his calendar to pursue those goals. In doing so, Jim exhibited mental toughness fundamental #4: prioritize the priorities.

PRIORITIZE THE PRIORITIES: If you want to achieve your product goals and live your vision of self-image, process goal completion must be the priority each and every day.

Good process goals capture the fundamentals for achieving your dreams. Only through conscious prioritizing will you develop enough accountability to improve your performance and achieve your win.

Prioritize or Perish

It's pretty obvious that if you don't emphasize what's important, you will never get where you are trying to go. When you completed the work task exercise in the previous chapter, did you find, like so many do, that you weren't completing the most important tasks each day? Although we can come up with all kinds of excuses for why we don't do what's important, we're usually either allowing ourselves to get distracted or consciously or subconsciously steering around a stressful situation. Either way, your "avoidance of the important" causes the disparity between what you want and what you have.

Being Distracted by the Unimportant

> We live in digital time. Our rhythms are rushed, rapid fire, and relentless, our days are carved into bits and bytes. . . . We race through our lives without pausing to consider who we really want to be or where we really want to go. We're wired up, but we're melting down. . . . We survive on too little sleep, wolf down fast foods on the run, fuel up with coffee, and cool down with alcohol and sleeping pills.[1]
>
> —Jim Loehr, *The Power of Full Engagement*

In this day and age it is normal to feel overwhelmed by information overload, multitasking, and extreme time management. "Urgent" items inundate our daily to-do lists. It isn't uncommon to spend hours putting out the fires that masquerade as important issues—hours that could have been spent developing long-term solutions to truly important problems. An executive has to cancel a manufacturing strategy session because a machine is broken again and all hands are on deck to figure out a repair. A customer service manager spends 80 percent of her time handling complaints about hold times instead of identifying and integrating a new scheduling system. A parent has to stop what he or she is doing several times a day to break up a fight and then feels there's never enough time to implement a comprehensive plan to teach the kids to work it out themselves. As Stephen Covey, who was recognized as one of *Time* magazine's 25 most influential Americans, puts it, "the noise of urgency creates the illusion of importance."[2]

I think you will find daily emergencies will cease to exist when you make the choice to stop responding to them. Letting yourself be blown by the wind of the seemingly urgent is simply unacceptable if you want to reach your potential. You have taken the time to identify truly what is most important on a daily basis: your process goals.

Now is the time to prioritize them so they get done. Does that mean some fires will have to burn themselves out without your involvement? Yes. Does that mean that you'll disappoint colleagues, customers, or family members because you don't always drop what you are doing to participate in their problems? Sure. Prioritizing your process goals doesn't mean that you will never help someone else out. It just means that you'll get to it after you've made sure you'll have time for *your* most important tasks.

Avoiding Unpleasant or Stressful Situations

Whether you are a salesperson trying to make more money, a CFO seeking to reconnect with your family, or a manager looking for a promotion to director, you need to have process goals and you will need to make the decision to prioritize them—even if the actions you must take are uncomfortable, unfamiliar, or even downright frightening.

It is demanding to stay committed to your process goals day after day because they will be mentally, emotionally, and, in some cases, physically difficult to execute. The truth is, the most important tasks in each of our days are also typically the same tasks we fear and avoid the most. Psychologists can come up with many reasons for why we tend to avoid what is most important; most of those reasons fall into either the "fear of failure" or "fear of rejection" bucket. Take financial advisor Steve's process goals of making 20 client calls per day even in times when the market has decimated value: it can get really old really fast to be rejected 20 times daily.

I will offer proven tools to help with your ability to execute at a higher level in Chapters 6, 7, and 8, but there will be times when the process won't produce immediate results. Even in those times, remember that completing process goals daily is the absolute best manner in which to control your destiny. Being relentless about process goal completion will put you in the position to avoid long-term slumps and unproductivity. On a daily basis, rally your energy and courage to tackle those daily goals that have the greatest influence on your performance and therefore success.

Getting Started on Greatness

Brian Tracy, a bestselling personal development author, calls the most important and most challenging tasks we need to complete daily our "big frog" tasks. Most people, he writes, choose to focus first on the nonimportant tasks (the little frogs) and save the big frogs for last. The problem is that if the big frogs are at the bottom of your to-do list, you will have a psychological tendency to find ways to procrastinate so that you won't have to face them. Saving the big frogs for last means that you will need the greatest courage and energy at the end of the day when you are most tired from spending countless hours completing tasks that may be urgent but not that important. By eating the big frogs first, you create energy and momentum through your early accomplishment of something that has true impact. This makes it easier to complete your less important tasks and hence your to-do list in its entirety. In addition, completing important tasks earlier in the day ensures that even if you don't complete all your daily tasks, you will have already checked off those that create the biggest impact.[3]

A marketing executive I work with said this about eating the big frogs first: "It's like swinging a weighted baseball bat: you get those tough things done first thing in the morning and then the rest of the day you feel like you are on top of the world. Everything feels lighter and easier once you check off those heavy goals."

Not only does eating the big frogs first give you energy for the day, it also helps you avoid procrastinating. If you're a boss, for instance, chances are that you put the most important conversations with direct reports off until late in the day. But by the end of the day, there will be plenty of excuses to avoid saying what needs to be said. Eat that big frog first thing in the morning, and you won't need to waste brain cells coming up with those excuses or worrying about what's coming next.

Undoubtedly, your big frogs are your process goals. How could anything be more important than putting them into action right away? To help people get those process goals done, I developed one simple yet effective rule: ETS—*emphasize the start.* Don't get ahead of yourself by thinking about how long it will take to finish your process goals. Instead, focus your mind on getting started. For instance, I've taught Steve not to focus on making 20 calls but rather to think just about making the first one. Once started, momentum is on his side.

The process goals will eventually deliver your dreams if you emphasize the start. And remember, ETS isn't just for your career process goals: it applies every bit as much to your personal process goals. Instead of thinking about riding the elliptical for 30 minutes, focus your energy on simply getting through the first 5 minutes. The rest will take care of itself.

Excuses: The Enemy of Accountability

When I ask people why they do not actually finish their daily process goals, I usually hear some pretty good excuses. It's easy to give yourself permission, or as I call it, a free pass, to justify not completing your process goals daily. Something "unavoidable" will always come up and give you a viable excuse, *if* you allow it to.

It's especially hard to avoid the trap of excuses when your goals themselves seem to conflict with each other. Let's take, for example, Leo, an editor at a major market newspaper and one of my clients. One of his product goals was to publish his second book. He decided on a process goal of two hours per day of book writing. However, with the critical demands of his work at the newspaper, he knew that if he didn't get his book writing done before reporting to the office, he wouldn't get it done. Therefore, he decided to eat his big frog early and work on the book each day from 4:30 to 6:30 A.M.

A month or so into this plan, Leo e-mailed me to say that of late he hadn't been able get his writing done because of complications with his children; he had three kids under the age of six. When I e-mailed back expressing my genuine concern about the welfare of his family, he answered that his four-year-old had been waking up at 5:00 A.M. for the last few weeks, effectively killing his morning writing slot.

Of course, his children were and should have been a priority. So how could he have prioritized more than one thing at a time? The answer lies in channel capacity, a concept we've run into already that says it's possible to prioritize up to three things at a time. I'm not suggesting Leo should have multitasked writing and caring for his wakeful child; the latest research on multitasking says it's not as good of an idea as previously believed. Two other very workable solutions to his writing conundrum rose to the surface within a few minutes of our searching for a workable solution. He realized he could ask his wife to help out more in the mornings, or he could let his son have his own hour of computer time on his favorite word and math program. These seemed very doable and logical, right?

Two more weeks went by, and Leo still hadn't implemented either solution so he could resume his process goal completion. Why, when we came up with the solution to completing his writing so easily, did he not make it happen? The answer is simple: Leo, like most of us, had been looking for justifiable excuses to avoid eating his big frogs. What could be more justifiable than taking care of a young child?

Resist the urge to allow yourself to use an excuse when it comes to process goal completion, even though the excuse is justifiable, and even though you will want to do so. You'll need to show discipline, a topic you'll learn more about in Chapter 10, and creativity at times to complete these important tasks. The trick is to develop the no-excuse mentality. Make it a habit to turn off the cell phone and shut down your e-mail for the time it takes you to complete your daily process goals. Do not, under any circumstance, allow yourself a "free pass" when it comes to daily process goal completion. Do not let anything interrupt those tasks that are most critical for growth in the important areas of your life. Find a way, no matter what, to prioritize your daily process goals, even when you have a viable excuse to justify not doing so.

Emphasizing your process goals will require energy, courage, and plain hard work. As Norman Vincent Peale, famous author of *The Power of Positive Thinking,* intones, "Nothing of great value in this life comes easily." If your process goals were easy to complete each and every day, then they probably wouldn't produce much in terms of greatness.

The Perfect Schedule

Imagine for a moment how great it would be to have the perfect schedule. What would that mean? How much would you work, and how much would you play? And how exactly would you prioritize your time? I love asking those questions and seeing my clients dream about what their lives could be. To be honest, a perfect schedule isn't a possibility for everyone. In fact, it's quite difficult to live your perfect schedule if you aren't the head honcho. I would, however, like you to begin answering these questions so you can start moving in the *direction* of the schedule that suits you perfectly precisely because it helps you to prioritize your priorities.

Hector is now a very successful dentist who oversees his three offices while living his perfect schedule each and every day, but it wasn't always the case. A few years ago, Hector decided that he was going to schedule his calendar rather than having his calendar schedule him, for that's exactly what had been going on for quite a long time. Hector loves his wife and four kids, and he is also very passionate about his work. Like many successful professionals with families, Hector found himself spending lots of time and energy trying to improve his career while managing to do the best he could with his family. The problem for Hector was that he didn't like the person he was becoming:

> *One day about three years ago, I realized I hadn't laughed— I mean really laughed—in a long, long time. That's when I knew something was off. I looked at my life and how my days were being spent, and it hit me that I was trying to make everyone else happy, but I was forgetting about myself and my priorities. I made a list of all the important things in my life, I included what I absolutely needed to do each day and*

week, and I also included things that I wanted to do each week. Then I decided to put it all in a schedule. It was my perfect schedule. I figured, hey, I have worked very hard to get where I am, and I deserve to live the life I want.

Hector went day by day and created his perfect schedule. He changed his office hours from 8:00 A.M. to 6:00 P.M. Monday through Friday and 9:00 A.M. to 12:00 P.M. most Saturdays to 9:00 A.M. to 5:00 P.M. Monday through Thursday and no Fridays or Saturdays. He scheduled time daily to complete his personal and professional process goals, and he also made a not-to-do list that forbade him from counterproductive tasks such as taking clients after 3:30 P.M. or responding to e-mail during family time. Essentially, he trimmed the fat: Hector stopped doing the activities that were time and energy drains and instead did only things that were essential or desirable.

Hector resegmented his client load by hiring two new dentists to handle all of the less-invasive dentistry. That move freed him up for the more interesting and profitable cases, thus causing an increase in his yearly profits. With the additional hours he had off from work, he spent more time doing the things *he* wanted to do: "I enjoy cooking a great deal, and I absolutely love cooking for my family. Now I get to have breakfast and dinner with my family five days a week. I get to work out, and I feel good about myself." What Hector found surprised him a great deal: by controlling his schedule, he was able to spend much more quality time with his wife and kids *and* be more successful at work *and* spend time on activities he enjoyed for himself. "The best part is," he says, "I am laughing again."

You can take steps to make your schedule more perfect, too. Even if you aren't able to completely restructure your work life, the mere exercise of thinking how you would if you could will help you set your priorities.

Take a few minutes and answer the following questions in the space provided.

What are three things you would like to do weekly for fun?

1. _____

2. _____

3. _____

What are three things you currently do weekly at work that should go on your "not-to-do list"?

1. _____

2. _____

3. _____

What are three things you currently do weekly at home that should go on your "not-to-do list"?

1. _____

2. _____

3. _____

What would your perfect schedule look like? Include time for process goal completion and time for activities from the first question.

DAY	5 A.M.	6	7	8	9	10	11	12	1 P.M.	2	3	4	5	6	7	8	9	10	11
Mon																			
Tue																			
Wed																			
Thu																			
Fri																			
Sat																			
Sun																			

Rituals Lock In Priorities

Whether you are able to make the leap to your perfect schedule or not, take a few minutes and *ritualize* some of the more important things you need to prioritize. You create a ritual when you get in the habit of behaving in certain ways consistently over time. I have found the only way of ritualizing in our busy schedules is to actually plug priority behaviors into our daily calendars.

> Please pull out your day planner or digital calendar right now and insert time slots into your schedule to complete every one of your daily process goals.

Usually when I make this suggestion, people look at me like I am joking. To be clear: *I am not joking, please get your calendar!*

Be realistic in estimating the time you need to fully complete your process goals. Be sure to prioritize your priorities by securing space early in your day for completion of your most important process goals and those big frogs you resist eating. Technology can help you here. Use the repeat function to prioritize a task into your schedule indefinitely. Use the alert function to schedule an alert that will remind you that it is process goal time. If you are a paper-calendar person, handwrite these appointments in your calendar for at least the next 12 months. Yes, it's that important.

As you are securing the daily time slots to complete all process goals, make the commitment to yourself that you will use the self-discipline required to work only on process goals during the time slots chosen. If completing process goals means you can't get to all the items on your to-do list, so be it. As long as you've checked off each process goal every day, you are demonstrating that you are prioritizing your priorities. Make the decision each and every day, without excuse, to start and complete your process goals, and you will see just how attainable greatness really is.

I cannot emphasize enough the importance of elevating your process goals to the level of appointments on your calendar. By treating your process goals as daily rituals, you will be much more likely to complete them and boost your self-confidence, increase your personal and professional productivity, and dramatically increase your chances of success.

Choose to Be Great

Mental Toughness Fundamental #4: Prioritize the Priorities.

If you want to achieve your product goals and live your vision of self-image, process goal completion must be the priority each and every day!

To the best of your ability, complete the following three tasks:

1. Identify the top three obstacles that make it difficult for you to fully complete your process goals on a daily basis (e.g., Mondays are difficult because I have to take my son to baseball practice, which ends my workday at 3:30 P.M.).

2. Identify one possible solution for each of the obstacles listed in question 1 (e.g., wake up at 5:00 A.M. on Mondays, and get 90 minutes of proposals and e-mail done before work begins).

3. Develop an accountability buddy: teach one person about process goals, and then make the commitment to send an e-mail to each other every Friday asking on a scale of 1 to 10 how well you have done with the completion of each process goal.

Accountability Through Self-Evaluation

Learn to Look in the Mirror Every Day

I walked into the arena with Tom Bartow, a man I had just met in person a few hours earlier. I had heard that Tom was a legend in the world of executive coaching; he had coached thousands of businessmen and businesswomen to achieve breakout success. Yet the soft-spoken humility I had witnessed up to this point didn't seem to match his reputation. As we made our way through security, I began to see a legend in action. Scores of Tom's current and former clients lined the hallway to shake hands with the man who had helped so many take their business success to the next level.

In front of a standing-room-only audience, Tom began his speech and immediately drove home his point. "You are going to survive," Tom's animated voice boomed through the air. Tom repeated the mantra but this time with more fervor:

You are going to survive. You have all just come through the second worst economy in history. You are still here and have clients who have believed in you during this period. You have what it takes to get to the next level. You have proven over the past months that you have the strength to fight through the toughest of times. Could a weak person have made it through this? *You are going to survive.* So I have a question for you: Why not win?

Tom Bartow was destined to coach. His father, Dr. Gale T. Bartow, built his own career as an extremely successful high school basketball coach before becoming one of the nation's top school superintendents. His uncle, Gene Bartow, earned a place in the National Collegiate Basketball Hall of Fame for coaching teams that included the basketball powerhouse UCLA Bruins; he later held executive positions with the NBA's Memphis Grizzlies. Gene took over the reins at UCLA after legendary coach John Wooden retired, and in that capacity, he introduced his nephew Tom, who had just started to follow in his uncle's professional footsteps, to Coach Wooden. Captivated with Coach Wooden, Tom learned how to motivate and inspire. Under Coach Wooden's ongoing tutelage, Tom developed the reputation as a coach who could turn underperforming college basketball teams into winners. Yet their relationship surpassed the usual mentor-mentee connection. Tom and Coach Wooden became very close friends—in fact, Coach Wooden counted Tom as one of his closest friends.

Eventually Tom left basketball and became an extremely successful financial advisor before finally moving on to executive coaching. One of the most impactful Wooden-inspired principles Tom teaches is the habit of evaluation. As Tom and I got to know each other, he shared the following vignette with me:

I was with Coach Wooden who was 93 at the time, and he was doing a talk for some of the top business executives who

> had traveled across the country to hear him speak about lead-
> ership. After he wrapped up his obviously compelling talk,
> the audience jumped up in a standing ovation and cheered
> loudly. Coach Wooden began walking off the stage, and I
> could tell he wasn't pleased. As I helped him down from the
> stage, I notice he was shaking his head and muttering under
> his breath, so I asked what in the world was the matter.
> Coach responded, "I wasn't at my best today."

As Tom wrapped up the story, he looked me square in the eyes and asked, "If you don't evaluate yourself, how in the heck are you ever going to know what you are doing well and what you need to improve?" Without giving me time to respond, he answered for me, "You won't!" I smiled, as I knew Coach Bartow was correct:

No evaluation = No awareness = No improvement
                  of how you
                  are doing

Most 90-year-olds content themselves with daily accomplishments like sharing a glass of lemonade with the grandkids and making it to the easy chair in time for the evening news. Not Coach John Wooden, even at the age of 93 not only was he advising some of the greatest business minds in the world, he also continued to self-evaluate his performance as a speaker. He never diluted his belief in self-evaluation: it remained as strong in his final years as it was during the time he coached some of the greatest college basketball teams in history.

Now that you know where you are trying to go (vision of self-image), have listed the specifics of what you need to do to get there (product and process goals), and have calendared time to prioritize your priorities, it's time to create an evaluation system that will motivate you and help keep you on the fast track for success. Mental toughness fundamental #5 is to complete daily performance evaluations.

COMPLETE DAILY PERFORMANCE EVALUATIONS:
Take the time on a daily basis to evaluate your personal
progress and effort, and you will inevitably learn to
achieve your win.

When you do, you will be accountable first and foremost
to yourself. You'll be able to look yourself in the mirror,
and you will like what you see looking back at you.

Performance Versus Perfectionist Evaluation

One of the little-known secrets of successful individuals
is that those who are most successful evaluate themselves
daily. Daily evaluation is the key to daily success, and daily
success is the key to success in life and career. While most
successful individuals conduct some form of consistent personal evaluation, those who are highly successful perform
what I call a *performance* evaluation on themselves. Performance evaluations include three very distinct components:

1. What is being done well
2. What needs to be improved
3. How improvements will be made

Although performance evaluations sound simple, very
few people actually evaluate themselves along these lines.
Most people personally assess themselves with a perfectionist evaluation. Perfectionist evaluations tend mostly to
emphasize where people see themselves fall short. A few
years back, I worked with a bright young man, whom we
will call Bill, who had moved up quickly in his mechanical
engineering company. He appeared to have a very promising future ahead of him. When I first began working with
Bill, he had just been asked to take over the leadership of
a team that was underperforming. Three months later, I

asked Bill to evaluate his team's performance for the quarter. He commented on how poorly he felt he had done. He told me that he had come up short on holding his team accountable for results. He said he had failed to offer professional development opportunities for the members of his team to grow intellectually, and he had misfired on his decision to propose a change in the current incentive and compensation plan.

I then asked Bill if anything positive had happened in the last quarter. His response of no was a warning sign that Bill operated with a perfectionist mentality. You've seen this before: people do something well but write it off as something they already expected of themselves, and when they come up short, they beat themselves up for their inadequacies. The perfectionist mentality is a great recipe for inconsistent performance. Bill needed to make some changes, or he wouldn't last long in his position. Unfortunately, Bill firmly believed that his perfectionist mentality had led to his prior success, and he refused to adopt the performance evaluation method I introduced to him. Within 16 months, Bill was released from his company.

Imagine for a moment that you have a boss who overlooks all of the things you do well and notices only the tasks you don't complete or the times you screw up. Imagine working for someone who neglects to mention any of your strong points. How long would it take for you to build up resentment and anger toward your boss? Not long, I assure you. Realize that when you subject yourself day in and day out to your own perfectionist evaluation, you will begin to feel the same way toward yourself as you would toward the imaginary boss. Only a perfect person will find the perfectionist mentality to be an effective form of evaluation. And we all know that no one is perfect.

Ben Hogan, one of the greatest golfers of all time, said the following about perfection, "I stopped trying to do a great many things perfectly, because it had become clear

in my mind that this ambitious overthoroughness was neither possible . . . or even necessary."[1]

Many of my clients ask me to help them "not get too
high or too low." The truth is, what they really want is
help with just one side of that coin—not getting too low.
The best method I have found to create that even keel of
success is ditching the perfectionist evaluation in favor of
a performance evaluation. Performance evaluations force
individuals to (1) give themselves credit where credit is due
and (2) relentlessly search for improvement. Remember the
discussion in Chapter 2 about the thermostat nature of self-
image? If you think of yourself in a positive light, you are
more likely to perform in positive ways and vice versa. The
same mechanism works with the evaluation you give yourself. When you give yourself credit where credit is due,
you actually reinforce your likelihood of continuing the
positive behavior. Think about it: if you do something well
and then make a mental note, "Hey, I just did something
well!" it underscores the positive and makes it more likely
that you will remember to do those positive things in the
future.

Performance evaluation isn't just about patting yourself
on the back for the things done well. Being aware of what
you *don't know* is one of the greatest facets of intelligence,
and each performance evaluation forces you to continually search for the means to *know* more. Looking at what
you want to improve is far more beneficial than focusing
on the times you screwed up. Expectancy theory—covered
in the introduction of this book—tells us that the image
we focus on expands. Continually thinking about what
you are doing poorly, as do perfectionists, will undoubtedly cause more underperforming behavior. Conversely,
if you can shift your evaluation to lock your mind on the
improvements needed, then those improvements will be
much more likely to occur.

The combination of *giving yourself credit where credit is due* and *relentlessly searching for improvement* will not only develop your self-image but also help you identify where you need to work harder or differently.

The Success Log: Knowing the Score Every Day

A great way of *training* your mind to focus on performance rather than perfection is to complete a written success log daily. I ask every athlete and businessperson I work with to commit to this practice. When you make the effort to ritualize the daily completion of a success log, you will train your mind to think in a new way—a way that leads to increased self-confidence and improved performance, and discourages you from conducting a perfectionist evaluation that in turn will lead to lowered self-concept, frustration, burnout, and poor performance.

A success log consists of the following six questions:

1. What three things did I do well today?

_____

_____

_____

2. What is my number one most needed improvement for tomorrow?

_____

_____

_____

3. What is one thing I can do differently to help make the needed improvement?

_____

_____

_____

4. On a scale of 1 to 10 (10 being total completion of each process goal), how well did I do today with the completion of my priority 1 process goals?

1   2   3   4   5   6   7   8   9   10

5. On a scale of 1 to 10, how well did I do today with the completion of my priority 2 process goals?

1   2   3   4   5   6   7   8   9   10

6. On a scale of 1 to 10, how well did I do today with the completion of my priority 3 process goals?

1   2   3   4   5   6   7   8   9   10

Completing this log won't take a lot of time. You want to make brief entries, with detailed specificity that I call level two detail. Level two detail greatly increases the positive impact of the success log and occurs when your answers are detailed enough to lead you to focus in on a specific point in time. The following examples show level two detail.

Pharmaceutical Account Executive: Career Priority

1. What three things did I do well today?

Had a lot of activity: made 10 current client and 5 prospect calls.

Arranged call schedule so that I spent less than 2 hours driving.

Covered all key points in a presentation to a doctor before he had to get back to patients.

2. What is my number one most needed improvement for tomorrow?

Improve my closing rate by offering a solid response to pricing concerns.

3. What is one thing I can do differently to help make the needed improvement?

Practice by creating a script of a new response, and practice three times in front of a colleague (Jim).

Accountant: Family Priority

1. What three things did I do well today?

Woke my son up and sang happy birthday to him before I left for work; dedicated 10 minutes during a time he usually doesn't see me.

Made it home by 6:45, before family had finished eating dinner.

Gave both kids a bath while my wife cleaned the kitchen.

2. What is my number one most needed improvement for tomorrow?

Helping my daughter with her math homework by sitting with her in my office with the door closed to distractions for 30 minutes.

3. What is one thing I can do differently to help make the needed improvement?

Carve out time right after dinner by asking my wife if she's OK to clean up and get our son in the bathtub while I help with the homework.

CEO of a Construction Company: Relationship with Self Priority

1. What three things did I do well today?

Didn't eat junk food; did not have chips and soda in the car between job sites.

All day I took the stairs instead of the elevator.

In bed at 10 P.M., had a full eight hours of sleep last night.

2. What is my number one most needed improvement for tomorrow?

Drink more water by aiming for 80 fluid ounces over the course of the day.

3. What is one thing I can do differently to help make the needed improvement?

Carry a water bottle with me in the truck. Refill it at each job site.

Although these success logs are specific to one priority at a time, feel free to answer across priorities if you so choose. One success log per day will suffice. Remember, answering the success log questions with level two detail will greatly enhance your mind's efficiency as it begins thinking through the performance evaluation lens. The more specific you are with your answers, the more quickly you will develop unwavering self-confidence and the more relentless you will be in creating the growth needed for optimal success.

Most, if not all, of the individuals I work with believe in the success log so much that they will not consider their day officially finished until they have completed it. Susan, an executive with a luxury hotel chain, had the following to say about success logs:

They are the key to the whole thing. The three or four minutes a day it takes to complete the success log has more impact on my personal and professional success than anything else. Doing success logs daily reminds me to focus on my process goals and forces me to realize that bad days aren't the end of the world and that I can always do something to improve.

Think about it: if at the end of every day you know you have to identify three things you have done well, you will eventually start thinking about what those three positives are throughout the day. By training your mind to be aware of your small successes throughout the day, you will build your self-image bit by powerful bit.

The most successful professional athletes have short memories when it comes to remembering losses. They have learned that the worst way to spend their time is dwelling on the negative. It's no exaggeration to say that every second they spend focusing on poor past performance *causes* more trouble in the future. The same concept works in businesses and our personal lives. Train your mind to emphasize what needs to be improved rather than allowing your thoughts to swirl around the previously made mistakes. That's why it is equally important to daily answer the question, "What is the one greatest need for improvement tomorrow?" By continuing to search for growth, you develop in yourself the attack mentality that high-level success requires. I've already said that greatness takes work, and I'll say it again. If you want to achieve greatness, push yourself to the limits of your potential by continuously looking for improvements.

The third question, "What is one thing I can do differently to help make the needed improvement?" will get you in the habit of identifying the *process* necessary to make the improvements you have identified. It is not enough merely to determine what you want to accomplish. True growth occurs as a result of identifying the daily behaviors needed to make the improvement a reality. Forcing yourself to write down one thing you will do differently to grow will help your thought patterns shift from the normal *outcome* thinking to the more powerful *process* thought pattern. Once process thinking becomes a habit, you will find life becomes much more enjoyable and you will have far more control over your success.

Questions 4, 5, and 6 will remind you to keep a daily focus on those process goals you have set for yourself. I have found that without the written daily completion of a success log, individuals over time forget their process goals. Complete a success log each day, and keep those goals on your mind.

For practice, fill in the previous blank success log. If not much has happened yet in your day today, answer by reflecting on yesterday.

Then commit to keeping a success log for one week. Make copies of the work sheets available for download on my website at http://www.jasonselk.com. Keep a stack of blank success logs right on your desk or nightstand, or have the blank file on your computer desktop. Fill out the success log as the last thing you do each day before leaving the office or just before going to bed.

Leave the completed log where you can see it first thing the next day. After rereading what you wrote the previous day, place your completed success logs in a special file that you can review quarterly if you so desire.

After a particularly tough day, you may find that the last thing you want to do is fill out your success log, but that is precisely when the process will be most valuable. If, after a week of keeping success logs you don't feel it is helping you become more structured, focused, and organized, stop doing them. The last thing I would want you to do is waste your time, but I think you will find, as most have, that it is well worth your time and effort.

Quarterly Evaluation: Sticking with Reality

In addition to ritualizing daily evaluation, you need to plan for quarterly evaluations. Even though mental toughness fundamental #5 refers to *daily* evaluation of process goals, and three-month evaluations of product goals are different, these major check-in points represent a very important step in completing the self-evaluation system. Having quarterly evaluations positively impacts the power of your daily evaluations because it will not only help you focus on the daily actions but also remind you of your progression toward the big goals. In addition, quarterly evaluations will help you learn the difference between a *reality evaluation* and *potential evaluation.*

REALITY EVALUATION: An evaluation that considers actual results.

POTENTIAL EVALUATION: An evaluation that consists of an aspiration about what the results could or should be.

Unfortunately, many individuals allow themselves to conduct self-evaluations based on potential rather than actual results. For example, Antonio, a commercial real-estate broker I coach, had a product goal of closing 12 deals. At his six-month goal evaluation, I asked him how he was doing, and he said, "Great, everything is lining up to achieve the goal." His potential evaluation included a description of "two deals that were as good as closed" and "two additional deals that were looking very promising." When I asked for his reality evaluation, he admitted he had actually closed only four deals in the first six months. At that pace, he would end the year with only eight deals closed, and he would underperform on his goal by 33 percent (Goal of 12 – 8 achieved = 4 short; 4 = 33 percent of 12).

The importance of reality evaluations is probably the most valuable lesson I have learned from working with professional athletes. The truth of the matter is that in professional sports if you don't produce results, then you won't be a pro for long. The same goes for my position with the Cardinals: if the players I work with don't perform better because of my working with them, then I won't be working with them for long. John Mozeliak, the team's general manager, has made it very clear to me that if I want to keep my job with the Cardinals, I better help players produce results. If I went to John and said that the players are "on the verge of playing better" or that the "players' performance looked promising," my guess is that he would reply with a pink slip.

When you do your evaluations (whether daily or quarterly), use only the true reality of results and avoid letting your mind make judgments based on potential. In life and business, potential success or the promise of a deal often fail to come to fruition. Basing your self-evaluations solely on *actual* results will give you a much better indication of when you need to change your approach or just plain work harder. Evaluating merely the potential of success will drain your motivation for change because you're telling yourself that your win is already in the bag.

Using a true reality-based evaluation led Antonio to decide he needed to make changes if he was going to achieve his 12-sale product goal for the year. He decided to increase by 40 minutes per day the amount of time and energy he spent on his process goal of prospecting for new business. As a result, he ended up closing 14 deals in that year.

If you are not on track at each of your quarterly evaluations, using the same process goals will not produce much of a difference in terms of product goal results. So in that case, change or adjust at least one of your process goals related to the product goal that's coming up short. For example, if Antonio had already closed six or more sales at his second quarter evaluation, he would have been in great shape. Six sales is exactly where he needed to be halfway through to eventually hit his product goal of 12. There would have been no need for change in his process goals. However, four sales at the midway point would have put him at 66 percent of the way there and thus would have necessitated an adjustment of at least one process goal.

Just as you need to dedicate time in your schedule to complete your process goals and success logs, you need to enter time for quarterly evaluations on your calendar.

Identify four goal evaluation dates at which you will evaluate your progress on your product and process goals. Set your first goal evaluation date approximately 3 months from now, the second goal evaluation 6 months from now, the third 9 months from now, and the fourth—you guessed it—12 months from now.

Goal Evaluation Date 1: _____

Goal Evaluation Date 2: _____

Goal Evaluation Date 3: _____

Goal Evaluation Date 4: _____

When I say to set these dates, I mean that you should open your calendar or day planner right now and actually schedule 20 minutes on a specific day, at a set time on each of those dates, to complete the quarterly goal evaluation process described next. If you don't put these dates on your calendar, you're likely to forget them.

Follow these steps to evaluate yourself at each of the four quarterly goal evaluation dates you just scheduled:

1. **Using a reality-based evaluation, assess exactly where you are on each one of your three product goals.** On a scale of 1 to 10, using a reality-based evaluation, calculate how on track you are.

   1   2   3   4   5   6   7   8   9   10

   - If you are 90 to 100 percent on track, *great!* There is no need to change any of your process goals.
   - If you are less than 90 to 100 percent on track with your product goals, adjust at least one of your process goals.

2. **Determine on a scale of 1 to 10 how well you have done during the previous three months on the completion of your process goals.** Some very self-aware people can conduct a good self-assessment subjectively. For your first few quarters, however, I recommend that you pull out your old success logs and look at your daily scores on questions 4, 5, and 6 to honestly calculate your completion percentage as an indication of your score. At the third quarter, take a guess before you calculate the completion percentage. If your estimate is close, then know going forward

that you can complete a reality evaluation without a backup. If you're off, keep using your success logs until you indeed can make a good reality-based evaluation without them.

1   2   3   4   5   6   7   8   9   10

- If you score yourself a 9 or better on average across all process goals, reward yourself in some way within the next seven days. Try something small but enjoyable (steak dinner, message, new pair of shoes you have had your eye on, etc.)— even if you're not necessarily on track with your product goal. It may sound as if I am letting you off the hook, but I am not. I am simply acknowledging the reality that prioritizing your process goals will do much more to increase your chances of long-term happiness and success than focusing on product goals alone.
- If you score yourself less than a 9 on average across all process goals, recommit to your process goals. Reprioritize your calendar or make some change that will allow you to score higher on process goal completion next time around. Remember that your process goals are essentially the key to you achieving your win.

3. **Within seven days, follow through with your reward for completing process goals even if you are not 100 percent on track with your product goals.** Process is the priority! Rewarding yourself for committing to the process helps you start to create an effort-based definition of success that can really improve your motivation and work ethic while reducing counterproductive pressure. Rewards serve as a concrete reminder that you are great. The more you believe in your ability to achieve greatness, the more your confidence grows; the more confidence you have, the easier it will be to achieve success.

Look in the Mirror and See Accountability

Another accountability exercise I want you to work on is called "15 seconds of accountability." Each morning I would like you to look at yourself in the mirror—specifically, I want you to look yourself in the eyes. Chances are if you are an accountable person, you will feel fairly comfortable looking at yourself for such a long period; however, if you aren't doing well with accountability, 15 seconds may feel like an eternity. Get in the habit of looking into the mirror daily to better get in touch with who you are and who you are trying to become.

Tom Bartow uses quarterly evaluations and success logs with his clients because he knows the importance of self-evaluation. Tom learned from Coach Wooden a long time ago that people who don't evaluate themselves cannot possibly know what is going well and what needs to be improved. Make the commitment to the daily and quarterly performance evaluations, and you will be well on your way to developing your accountability and becoming the person you so desire to become.

Choose to Be Great

Mental Toughness Fundamental #5: Complete Daily Performance Evaluations. *Take the time on a daily basis to evaluate your personal progress and effort, and you will inevitably learn to achieve your win.*

To the best of your ability, complete the following three tasks:

1. Go to http://www.jasonselk.com to download work sheets from the *Executive Toughness* tab. Print off 30 success logs and four quarterly evaluations, and store them in a file folder that you will keep either on your nightstand or in an easily accessible place on your desk.

2. Find the nearest private mirror, and look at yourself. As you look deep into your own eyes, ask yourself just how accountable you are currently and how accountable you want to become. While doing so, identify one specific way to improve your current level of accountability.
3. Find someone you trust, and teach that person how to use success logs and quarterly evaluations to help him or her increase accountability.

DEVELOPING EXECUTIVE TOUGHNESS CHARACTERISTIC 2

Focus:
Improving Execution and Consistency

CHAPTER

6

Preparation

Control Your Emotions, Control Your Performance

On an intellectual level, Eric knew that he needed to motivate and empower his social media team members so they would perform better. Truth be told, he simply wanted to wring their necks. For the last 12 weeks, this arm of the marketing company that Eric ran had been underperforming. They had lost one major account, and a second was expressing displeasure due to social media results. Today, Eric was flying to Dallas to address the situation.

Eric had become CEO of one of the most successful marketing firms in the country because of his work ethic, creativity, and ability to inspire innovation. Over the years, he had impressed even himself with his ability to remain cool under fire in a company that experienced tremendous growing pains as it became an international marketing giant and landed major accounts with companies like Anheuser-Busch, Johnson & Johnson, and Whole Foods.

As Eric sat on the plane replaying the mistakes his team had made over the last few weeks, he felt his blood pressure and anger rise. Eric initially felt like writing down all the problems resulting from his team's recent lackadaisical performances. He wanted to assign blame to each and every individual who had made mistakes. However, what Eric actually did while sitting on that plane was quite the opposite. He took a few deep breaths and forced himself to calm down. Yes, the team needed a wake-up call, but Eric knew that getting angry and throwing a fit in front of his team—a team that, outside of the last 12 weeks, had proven worthy over the past few years—would probably make things progressively worse rather than better. Indulging himself by giving the team a tongue-lashing was probably not the best way for him to accomplish his goal of improved performance.

After calming himself down, Eric wrote down the following five questions that he would ask each member of his social media team:

1. In the last 12 weeks, on a scale of 1 to 10, how much effort have you put into being great at your job?
2. In the last 12 weeks, on a scale of 1 to 10, how have you done with results at your job?
3. What are the top two or three strengths of this division?
4. What is the number one greatest need for improvement within this division?
5. What is one thing you can do differently that could help make the needed improvement?

As the plane began its descent, Eric again spent a few minutes getting his emotions under control. Eric visualized himself in the upcoming meeting. He saw himself getting to the point quickly while remaining calm and focused. Within an hour of landing, Eric was in the Dallas office's large conference room:

I was sitting there watching members of the team come in. I remember three of them were joking and horsing around as they entered. I was ready to roll some heads, and here they were in their own little world. I could feel myself almost lose it. Thankfully, I knew what to do. I took a couple of deep breaths, gave a 60-second summary of the problem, and then asked the team to answer each of the five questions. We spent the next three hours discussing what needed to change and what each person was going to contribute. Each person clearly identified his or her primary role on the team. We had really never done that before. It was a very productive meeting—much more productive than if I had gone in there with guns blazing.

Long before the meeting that day in Dallas, Eric knew that anytime he was running a meeting he needed to control his emotions.

I was really worked up on the plane, but staying under control helped me prepare and stay focused. Even right before the meeting began, I felt myself getting agitated, and I knew to take a few deep breaths and to calm down. I did a good job of holding steady, and it was a good thing: in the year since that meeting, that team has probably been our most effective group.

Eric used several preparation techniques to improve his performance. Typically, *performance* is associated with an athletic feat or being on a stage. I think of *performance* in broader terms. Each time you make a sales pitch, facilitate a meeting, or participate in a performance review, you are performing. Think about it: for nonathletes, these business performances are every bit as important to success as throwing the game-winning touchdown is to an NFL quarterback. The sooner you come to view your workday as a performance, the sooner you'll understand how to apply mental tools to help you elevate that performance to a leadership level.

One of the most productive methods of increasing focus and hence performance success is learning how to control your ideal arousal state (IAS). Sometimes I hear snickers around a room when I use the word *arousal*; ideal arousal seems to bring forth even more adolescent thoughts. Despite the fact that our society has highjacked the word *arousal* by linking it to sex, this word perfectly captures the physical and psychological state associated with performance, so I'm going to use it.

AROUSAL: The extent to which nerves and emotions are engaged and on alert.

You know a deer is aroused when it locks its eyes, pricks up its ears, and freezes while it scans the surroundings for predators. You may experience performance arousal as feeling pumped up with potential energy: your heart beats faster, and you are aware, ready to rumble, psyched, maybe even on edge. I use a 10-point scale to measure IAS, with 1 reflecting a performance while half asleep, and a 10 performing at a thousand miles per hour. A person typically doesn't want to be a 1 or a 10 on the IAS but rather some number in between that feels more like the perfect symphony of calm, aggressive, and confident.

Only a small amount of pressure is needed to dramatically affect heart rate or arousal. This phenomenon is commonly referred to as performance anxiety. Performance anxiety can cause you to be too high on your 1 to 10 arousal scale (heart jumping out of your chest and mind racing), and it can also lead you to be too low on the arousal scale (lethargic and lackadaisical), which also can derail your performance. To counter performance anxiety and maintain your focus, it is essential to learn to control your IAS. That's why mental toughness fundamental #6 is to learn to control your arousal state.

CONTROL YOUR AROUSAL STATE: Learn to control your arousal state and cause your confidence to build, your brain to function more effectively, and your successes to grow.

The keys to controlling your arousal state are preparation and confidence: the more prepared you are, the more confident you will be, and hence the more likely you will be to maintain your IAS. Before you can control your arousal state, you need to work on a couple of preparatory building blocks. The first block is *identifying* the ideal arousal state for your three most important performances. The second block is physical well-being, and the third is cognitive preparation. With each of these building blocks firmly in place, you have the knowledge that you are prepared and ready. That knowledge will naturally produce confidence. And as we've seen before, when you give yourself positive messages, you increase your chances for success. Let's work on these building blocks, and then I'll show you how to control your arousal state to develop focus and drive high performance.

Preparation Block 1: Identifying Your Ideal Arousal State

A critical first step in controlling arousal is to know in advance of performance what your IAS actually is. Your IAS will vary according to the nature of the task at hand. Some tasks will require a higher IAS than others. For example, Eric may want to be a 7 on his 10-point IAS scale to exhibit enthusiasm and positive energy when doing large group presentations, while an IAS of 5 may allow him to be more attentive during one-on-one performance reviews. There are many reasons why your IAS may change across tasks. As you identify your IAS for each of the three most important work tasks you identified in Chapter 3, trust your own instincts. Look back at the times when you performed really well at the task in question and remember where you were on the IAS scale during those performances. If facilitating meetings happens to be one of your three most important tasks and you facilitated a great meeting last month while at an 8, then 8 may serve as your IAS number for this task.

Let me use Steve, the financial advisor whose mental toughness journey we've been following, again as an example. He lists his three most important work tasks as the following:

1. Client contact
2. Prospect new business
3. Identify referred lead prospects

For Steve, these tasks differ in the amount of emotional energy they require. Steve feels he is most effective during client contacts and prospecting new business when his IAS is a 6, while he likes to slow himself down to a 4 when identifying new referred leads.

Take a moment now and review the three top work tasks you identified in Chapter 3. Think back to the times when you were successful in those tasks, and estimate your IAS during those performances.

Then to the best of your ability, identify your IAS number for each of those tasks. Remember that the IAS is the level of energy and attentiveness you need to perform at your best, where 1 is being half asleep and 10 is going a thousand miles per hour. Your IAS should feel like the perfect level of calm, confident, and aggressive all at the same time.

Work task 1: IAS

| 1 | 2 | 3 | 4 | 5 | 6 | 7 | 8 | 9 | 10 |

Work task 2: IAS

| 1 | 2 | 3 | 4 | 5 | 6 | 7 | 8 | 9 | 10 |

Work task 3: IAS

| 1 | 2 | 3 | 4 | 5 | 6 | 7 | 8 | 9 | 10 |

While it can be a bit tough to define work tasks related to noncareer life priorities, you can use this same approach in your personal life. If one of your process goals is helping your child with homework, for instance, you can look back at past experience to determine the IAS associated with an effective session: if you're too keyed up (high IAS), you may make your child nervous, and if you are too emotionally spent (low IAS), you won't emit enough energy to motivate and inspire the budding scholar.

Preparation Block 2: Physical Well-Being for Increased Performance

In the business world, the physical aspect of performance isn't about being in spectacular shape. Instead, it's about being healthy and fit enough to (1) control your emotions and (2) have the stamina to maintain focus and energy throughout the day. When you make a commitment to the basics of good health—sleep, nutrition, and exercise—you will be physically able to do more. You will have more energy and stamina to complete your process goals. You'll reap cognitive benefits and increase your confidence. In short, you'll be in a better place to control your arousal state.

Get Some Sleep

Most adults perform better if they have somewhere between seven and nine hours of sleep per night. However, the latest research indicates that sleep requirements are actually unique to each individual.[1] A good night's sleep should leave you feeling energized and able to concentrate. Be honest with yourself about how many hours you truly need each night for optimal performance.

Once you have determined your optimal number of hours, make the commitment to getting just that. While it's not always easy to get a good night's sleep, the following steps can help you develop healthy sleep patterns:

- Follow consistent lights-out curfews and normal wake schedules respectful of the amount of sleep you require to optimally perform. Respect your lights-out curfew each evening just as you would if you were a professional athlete preparing for a big game.
- Get in the habit of reading for at least 15 minutes before the lights-out curfew to help prepare your mind for sleep.
- Avoid caffeine for more than six hours prior to the lights-out curfew.
- Avoid putting pressure on yourself to get to sleep. Trying to get to sleep makes it difficult to actually fall asleep. If your mind keeps your body awake, practice breathing slowly and use the awake time to visualize success and joy in the upcoming day. If you have physical issues that keep you awake, address them by seeing a doctor or other health professional and by following through on the advice given.

Eat Right

Nutrition is also very important for business performance. We have all heard the saying "garbage in, garbage out." Be sensitive to the fuel you put into your body by following these tips:

Tip 1: Deprioritize the joy and social aspects of eating. When you reduce the value you place on the non-nutritional aspects of eating, you are more likely to choose the best fuel for performance. Conducting business over meals, coffee, or drinks can put you in the position of eating or drinking too much of the wrong stuff. Each day, give yourself one meal to focus on the joy or social aspects of eating while emphasizing simple, good fuel in all other meals. Avoid between-meal meetings that involve food or drink, or opt for water or decaffeinated beverages during those times.

Tip 2: Watch fat gram intake. Carrying excess weight is counterproductive for performance. Hundreds of books set out weight-loss plans, but this is not one of them. In my opinion, a simple and effective way to limit weight gain is to reduce fat intake (aim for less than 40 grams of fat per day). Allow yourself only one free-pass meal per week, when you can let yourself indulge.

Tip 3: Avoid eating large meals prior to or during working hours. Large meals make you tired and diminish motivation. Brown bagging is popular these days, and it's the perfect way to control for smaller portions and healthier food choices. If you must go out to lunch, choose healthy alternatives or commit to portion control by leaving at least a third of the normal serving on your plate.

Put a Sweat On

According to Dr. John Medina, one of the world's foremost brain scientists and author of the bestselling book *Brain Rules*, if you want to be smarter, happier, healthier, and more popular, you need to exercise. Medina found that those who routinely get 30 minutes of cardiovascular exercise at least three times per week are smarter, are more able to concentrate, get along better with others, are less disruptive, have higher self-esteem, and have less anxiety. He and others put forth undeniable proof that exercise increases long-term memory, reasoning, attention, problem solving, and fluid intelligence tasks in a dramatic fashion.[2]

I encourage my clients to aim for increasing their heart rate to 130 beats per minute while completing 30 minutes of cardio exercise daily. Cardio at this level relieves stress, controls weight, and triggers the brain to release serotonin, a neurotransmitter that brings about feelings of happiness and satisfaction. In fact, getting the heart rate up to 130 beats per minute for 30 minutes rivals the therapeutic effects of many of the antidepressants on the market today and has only positive side effects, whereas antidepressants often introduce a host of negative side effects. Dr. Medina summarizes the benefits of cardiovascular exercise: "When combined with the intellectual benefits . . . we have in our hands as close to a magic bullet for improving human health as exists in modern medicine."

Simply put, 30 minutes a day of cardiovascular exercise is quite possibly the single greatest activity you can do to improve your mental, physical, and emotional health. If 30 minutes of cardio isn't currently one of your daily activities, I strongly encourage you to consider adding it in as one of your nine process goals.

Preparation Block 3: Intellectual Preparation for Business Performance

Another important building block of preparation is a master-level knowledge of your industry, customers, and competitors. Athletes like Payton Manning, Steve Nash, and Albert Pujols greatly contribute to their success by studying and knowing their game at a higher level than most of their competitors. To win in your field, study the Xs and Os of your industry and market so that you have a solid knowledge base. Because of the strong link between knowing your stuff and success, you may find that your career process goals include intellectual preparation. Steve's third process goal reads as follows: spend 90 minutes per day preparing and organizing.

For Steve, "preparing" includes market research, identifying referred leads, and keeping an eye on his competition, as well as time for his mental workout (we'll get to that in Chapter 8). "Organizing" is essentially another step of preparation, as it captures the time he spends qualifying leads, creating his call list for the day, and reviewing the account histories and files of the people he plans to call.

Michael Staenberg, president and cofounder of THF, the third-largest commercial real-estate company in the United States, believes that an individual simply can't compete unless he or she is willing to do the work to be prepared. Staenberg, who built THF (THF stands for *to have fun*) from the ground into a billion-dollar corporation, takes great pride in always being prepared. Michael once told me, "You need to understand who your client is and what you're trying to sell. The biggest thing to remember is money never leads the deal, but rather the right deal will lead to the money, and it's impossible to make the right deal if you haven't done your homework."

I fully agree with Michael that most people don't want to spend the time to be prepared. They won't take the time to learn about their clients, because they just want to get the deal done. I believe fewer than 10 percent of businesspeople actually spend daily and weekly time preparing. "A lot of owners get fat and happy; they want someone else to do the work for them and then they want to close the deal. But there is no substitute for doing the work yourself," Staenberg continues. He goes on to suggest that you don't have to spend hours upon hours each day to be prepared, "Instead, put *some* effort into preparation each day. You know if you're prepared or not, and the key is to be honest with yourself and be ready for every day."

I find, however, that many business professionals find personal preparedness quite difficult to assess. I suggest that all of my clients set aside at least half an hour per day to prepare for future success. The 30 minutes I prescribe could include anything from identifying the next day's call list (as in Steve's case) to reading the latest industry-specific updates to going over customer reviews. In any case, the key is to set the time aside and prioritize this commitment to future growth. Again, you should consider adding another process goal, *30 minutes of daily intellectual preparation*, to your list; but remember, you don't want to ever have more than nine total process goals. Allowing only nine process goals will help prioritize only the most productive tasks and keep life simple.

How Much Preparation Is Too Much Preparation?

At a certain point, you have to stop preparing and get in the game. I've highlighted three components of preparation, and I can imagine that you may feel that you could make a career out of being prepared for your career. So let's talk about the *right* level of preparation. Timothy Ferriss, author of the bestselling books *The 4-Hour Workweek* and *The 4-Hour Body*, believes you should identify the bare minimum amount of preparation needed to be successful. Ferriss calls this concept the "minimum effective dose."[3] The concept is simple: there's a point at which the amount of effort spent on preparation is the ideal amount for producing results. Intensity and consistency govern that ideal amount of effort. For example, if you were to spend eight hours every day with your spouse, you may experience an initial positive impact. However, anyone who has spent that much time with his or her spouse knows how quickly that duration can become counterproductive. Why? Typically, individuals will have difficulty maintaining the intensity or motivation needed to make the eight hours per day *quality* time. On the other hand, spending one hour daily of quality time with your spouse not only is more manageable within your schedule but also could allow for both of you to maintain intensity at a high enough level to produce positive results for the relationship.

The same is true for your preparation effort needed in business. Find the bare minimum of preparation you need to be successful. Are there five trade journals in your industry? If so, which one or two do you need to read to know what's going on? Have 300 customers? Which 20 are the most important for you to know in and out on a daily basis? Which 50 can you look at once a week? And which 230 can you take a look at once a month? Drowning in reports about the activity of 30 competitors? Which 3 should you follow on a daily basis?

Obviously, you'll run into periods when you need to put more energy into intellectual and physical preparation. A supply shortage may, for example, impact all of your customers, and you will need to prepare deeply for each and every customer interaction to explain the situation. If you're recovering from surgery, you may need to dedicate more time to sleep, nutrition, and exercise to restore your stamina.

A general partner at Edward Jones told me that he either knocks himself out with intellectual preparation or he ends up feeling guilty and anxious because he isn't doing it all. I suggested to him and will reiterate to you: it is literally impossible for you and other businesspeople to be everything to everyone at all times. When you try to know everything about every industry trend, every client, every competitor every day, you will fail. You'll ironically end up feeling the chronic anxiety associated with under-preparedness even though you have been spending hours preparing.

To avoid that anxiety, take the time to identify the bare minimum amount of preparation needed to achieve greatness, and then follow through on completion every day.

Control Your Arousal State to Develop Performance Focus

You now have your three preparatory building blocks:

- Identification of your IAS for each of your most important tasks
- Physical well-being
- Intellectual knowledge of your industry, customers, and competitors

Let's review: being prepared and confident is the key to controlling your arousal and hence performance. *Realizing* you are prepared ultimately leads to confidence. Committing to preparedness in the three building blocks will help you have the realization that you are prepared and ultimately will help you feel the confidence needed to control the arousal state and significantly increase your performance consistency. The physical domain is your most basic foundation. You need to have a strong physical platform to be able to control your emotions and reach your IAS. In other words, you need physical confidence to have emotional confidence.

Intellectual preparation works with physical preparation to give you an undeniable belief in yourself and your ability. When you know that you know your stuff, you can't help but feel confident. Add the knowledge of your IAS for the task at hand, and you have everything you need to tell yourself that, yes, you can perform and succeed.

With these forms of preparedness, you can use these tactics to bring your IAS to the correct level.

Once you have your three preparation blocks in place, start using them to better control your performance. Remember, your mind won't work nearly as effectively if you don't control your IAS *during* performance; therefore, be sure to invoke your IAS just *before* each performance begins. Whether it be a meeting with an important customer at work or spending quality time at home with a loved one, identify and get to your IAS to ensure your body and mind are working together to control success. To increase your IAS and gear up, try the following:

- Remember a specific time when you felt your IAS was optimal for the desired task.
- Visualize what the desired IAS feels like while completing the desired task.
- Elevate your heart rate through exercise. If you need an instant pick-me-up, find an empty room and do 10 push-ups or jumping jacks.

To decrease your IAS and calm down, try the following:

- Take a centering breath where you breathe in for six seconds, hold for two seconds, and exhale for seven seconds.
- Remember a specific time when you felt your IAS was optimal for the desired task.
- Visualize what the desired IAS feels like while completing the desired task.

The best performers are those who align their physical, intellectual, emotional, and mental domains. Your mental domain is represented by the thoughts in your mind: the stories you are telling yourself and the "videos" you are playing for yourself. Achieve your IAS *before* trying to enter mental focus, because if your arousal level is too high, your mind loses its ability for detailed thought. If your arousal state is too low, you will have difficulty being confident in the task at hand.

Remember when Eric was on the plane to Dallas and he was angry thinking about all the mistakes his team had made? His arousal state was unproductively high; he started to think about "rolling some heads" instead of coming up with workable solutions. Once he calmed his arousal down to a 6, he was able to come up with the five questions and take a more effective approach of empowering and motivating. Eric's 6 may be different from your 6 and my 6. But as long as each of us knows how our IAS scale is calibrated, we can make the appropriate adjustments. Eric's story emphasizes why you should have your IAS in place *before* you think about your strategy for success. Otherwise, your emotions will handicap your mental abilities.

When you are physically and intellectually prepared, you will be better able to remain calm, cool, and collected when the pressure is on. Identifying your IAS for your most important tasks and developing the ability to adjust your emotions to that level will give you a much better chance of using your mind to help you perform for success in service of all of your life priorities. Instead of saying or doing things in the heat of the moment and then regretting them, learn to control your IAS and put yourself in a position where you replace your biggest regrets with your greatest successes.

Choose to Be Great

Mental Toughness Fundamental #6: Control Your Arousal State. *Learn to control your arousal state and cause your confidence to build, your brain to function more effectively, and your successes to grow.*

To the best of your ability, complete the following three tasks:

1. Practice going through the IAS scale by feeling for 10 seconds each what IASs of 1, 3, 5, 7, and 9 feel like.
2. Practice feeling the IAS for your most important process goal for each of your top three priorities in life.
3. Teach a friend or colleague how to identify his or her IAS for his or her three most important work tasks.

CHAPTER 7

Script Your Way to Focus

Always Say the Right Thing

lfred Granum grew up in the small town of Amery in northwestern Wisconsin without much money. The son of a military man, Al's first job was in a local canning factory, where he earned 14 cents an hour. He learned early that "anyone who wanted to eat was expected to work." After graduating college and spending three years in the military, Al eventually took a job as an insurance salesman, but he struggled to make ends meet. Not wanting to remain poor, Al determined that he would be more successful if he always knew the right thing to say and said it right. In fact, he decided to script exactly what he would say to his clients in response to their lack of interest in his insurance products. He essentially hoped to always remain one step ahead of rejection.

Al made a pretty good living knowing his scripts; in fact, he became the most successful insurance salesman of all time. He went on to devote 25 years to studying the precise cause of a salesman's success, and his findings reinforced his belief in his early tactic: successful business-people need to know what they are going to say *before* they

123

say it. In fact, he wrote a training manual with dozens of scripts, including the following examples.

What a salesman should say if his initial attempt is met with resistance:

> *I see. (Pause.) I had no reason to believe you were in the market for any specific financial products just at this time. However, in these days of constantly changing tax and economic circumstances, our planning services have been of interest to many. Will you be in town next week?*

And in response to a second objection:

> *I understand. (Pause.) Nevertheless, the reasons for my wanting to connect are first, to have a chance to meet you and second, to review our services and get your thoughts on the subject. On that basis, would you object to seeing me next Thursday at 2:00 P.M.?*

And to a third rejection:

> *I see. (Pause.) However, circumstances do have a way of changing. Would you have any objection to my staying in touch with you and checking again at a later date?*

Al believed that the details of performance needed to be worked out and rehearsed *before* the actual performance. Remember from the previous chapter that performance in business isn't just about being in front of a customer or behind the podium: it's every interaction you have. Mental toughness fundamental #6 is to know your scripts.

KNOW YOUR SCRIPTS: Develop your focus by knowing and practicing what you are going to say—before you say it!

When you develop, practice, and use scripts, you will feel prepared and confident, and you will make a great impression that delivers results.

The Importance of Routine

Almost every athlete I work with scripts his or her entire competition day (including precompetition routine, during competition performance, and postcompetition celebration/ recovery). One prolific hitter with the St. Louis Cardinals describes part of his multisensory routine as follows:

I wake up thinking about baseball. As I go through my morning, the excitement I feel in my stomach makes me feel alive. I move through the morning waiting for it to be time to go to the park. When I finally get there, the smells of the clubhouse make me feel at home. The guys, the trainers, the coaches, and the skipper—it all feels like a family. Then I start going through the routine. I take my time and enjoy the preparation. Every game day it's the same: I watch videos with Chad and figure out my approach for the day; then I go to work. I know exactly how many swings I need to get ready. I know exactly what my swing feels like when it is right, and I know exactly what I need to do to make that happen. I have done it so many times that I don't even have to think about it anymore . . . but I do. I think about it every night as I am going to sleep. I feel the bat in my hands. I feel my stance, and I feel the tension that happens in the box. I focus on it going exactly how I want it to go the next day, and then when the next day comes, it all feels so right.

Successful athletes intrinsically understand and accept the importance of knowing down to the smallest detail what they need to do to deliver consistently great performances. Among teams of equal talent, winning and losing are determined in the preparation. Vince Lombardi, the legendary coach of the NFL's Green Bay Packers, led his teams to greatness by drilling plays again and again and again. His power sweep (a simple play that relied on the perfect execution of the fundamentals of blocking and teamwork) dominated pro football for 10 years. Lombardi told his team:

> Gentlemen, if we can make this play work, we can run the football. You think there's anything special about this sweep? Well, there isn't. It's as basic a play as there can be in football. We simply do it over and over and over. There can never be enough emphasis on repetition. I want you to be able to run this sweep in your sleep. If we call the sweep 20 times, I'll expect it to work 20 times . . . not 18, not 19.[1]

Lombardi made it work because he consistently and repeatedly took the time to practice the physical "script" until his team achieved mastery.

Because athletes perform with their bodies and minds instead of their voices and minds, their preperformance routines focus on physical scripts. In business, you perform mainly through communication, and so you need to focus your preparation on verbal scripts. When it is actually time to make that ever-important sales call, motivate your team, or deliver a presentation to the board, you are in a losing situation, even if you bring forth 100 percent effort at the moment of performance, if you haven't prepared yourself beforehand.

Given my long experience with top athletes in a variety of sports, I am continually surprised at how many people "wing it" in business, even at the highest levels. Case in point: I coach a well-known motivational speaker who told me that he is at his best when he "shoots from the hip" during his talks. I sat in on one of his presentations, and I was indeed captivated by his passion. However, I also noticed that he tended to veer off on tangents. After this presentation, he told me how disappointed he was that he had not been able to include one of his favorite stories because he had run out of time.

When I asked him how much of his talk was scripted, he replied that he had the first and last 60 seconds memorized. In between, he followed a scant outline. After a long discussion, my speaker client admitted that he would probably be more effective if he scripted the first 30 seconds of each major content point. When I asked him why he had not done so, he replied by saying, "I guess I had myself convinced I would sound like a robot if my speeches were totally scripted. But I'm probably just being lazy. The fact is, if I work on it, I'm sure I can deliver a script with passion."

I was sure he could, too. In fact, we were both correct. His visible passion and connection to the audience *increased* with scripting and practice, and so will yours. When you follow a script, you free up more of your conscious mind for sensing, absorbing, and attending to the details of your current environment. Following a well-written script, whether in a formal presentation or in a less formal interaction, will help you increase confidence and reduce the stress involved in coming up with just the right thing to say on the fly. Your main selling points have already been worked out, so you will greatly enhance your ability to think and communicate more clearly. Knowing what you want to say before you say it and then visualizing yourself successfully communicating with your audience will, in short, increase your focus and therefore the quality of your performance.

Identify Your Three Most Important Scripts

Remember channel capacity and the rule of threes? It applies here, too. Even though you have dozens of important interactions every day, you can't possibly develop and practice a script of each one. Instead, identify the top three most important scripts you will need to elevate your performance to the leadership level and achieve your win. Look at your process goals and determine which ones involve speaking with or to others. If you do not find three process goals that involve speaking, go back to your work task list for ideas. For example, if you are in sales and have a process goal about making calls to initiate new business, you may want to develop one script for a cold call, one for a referred lead call, and one for obtaining referred leads from current clients. If one of your main tasks is management, you may want to develop one for assigning projects, one for giving positive feedback, and one for giving critical feedback.

You'll find scripts particularly helpful in situations that can become uncomfortable or stressful. For example, just like many financial advisors, Steve had become hesitant to make calls to clients whose investments had lost money in the economic downturn. He knew he needed to make these calls to reach his income goal, but he had recently developed great disdain for this task. When I asked him to create a script for these tough calls, he wrote the following in about five minutes:

> *Good morning, Mr. Jones. I just wanted to call and let you know I am thinking about you. I know times have been tough, but I just want to let you know I am here if you need anything. I also want you to know there are new products that you may want to consider investing some of your money in (brief product overview). Which one of the products are you most interested in hearing more about?*

Take a few moments now to identify the top three situations in which specific scripts will help you achieve your business goals.

Situation 1: _____

Situation 2: _____

Situation 3: _____

If you are having trouble limiting your list to just three scripts to support your career-related product goals, decide which three to start with. Write them, practice them, and integrate them into your daily work. A few weeks from now, add another. Once that script fits like a glove, add another one, and so on.

Scripts can be equally useful to meet your nonwork goals. For example, you may have a script like the following to use with one of your children when he or she is having a difficult day:

How about if you tell me what is going on, and I will promise to help. [Pause while listening to the problem.] I can understand why you are upset. Life is sometimes tough, isn't it? I know I have said it a thousand times, but I am going to say it again: I love you. I think I can help. Let's see if we can come up with a couple of solutions to the problem—anything that can make your situation even a little bit better. I'll even go first: what do you think about [quick solution]? Your turn for the next one . . .

Writing Your Scripts

Once you know the situations in which you want to use scripts, writing them can be relatively easy and quick. Take a look at Al's examples at the beginning of this chapter for some prototypes. As you write, remember these tips and guidelines:

- To begin developing your script, imagine yourself in the specific situation and think, "What is the first thing I need to say?" Then move on to the second and so on until you have sketched out at least the first three things you need to say.
- Include only what is important. Leave the fluff out of your script so that it remains short and easy to memorize.
- Focus your scripts on the main goals or desired outcomes of the communication.
- Leave a space to drop in details pertinent to the specifics of the moment you are delivering the script.

Write down your three most important scripts. In the blank on the title line, insert the description of situations you just identified in the preceding exercise. A good way to improve your scripts is to record and listen to yourself going through each script, editing after each time you listen. By the time you have done this three times, your scripts should be in "performance shape." If you don't have time now to complete the scripts, at least write one sentence for each one. You can come back later and fill in the other sentences when you have more time.

Script for _____ :

_____

_____

_____

_____

_____

Script for _____ :

_____

_____

_____

_____

_____

Script for _____ :

_____

_____

_____

_____

_____

Use these same tips and process to script important touch points within presentations. Identify each of the main points in a presentation, and then script three sentences for each:

- One sentence to transition from previous main point to current point
- Two sentences to make the current main point

Even this minimal script will help you stay on topic, deliver all your key points, reduce your stress, and maintain your focus.

Practice Makes Permanent

Having scripts written and in the file isn't enough to develop focus and deliver leadership-level performance. Now that you know what you want to say, practice with passion and purpose so you can use the knowledge of what you want to say to your advantage. You need to be able to perform your scripts with efficiency and effectiveness, and to do so, you have to know them inside and out.

Practice until you can recite your scripts, *not* 19 out of 20 times, but as Coach Lombardi would say, *20 out of 20 times.* Practice in front of the mirror in the morning, while you are driving, when you are in an elevator by yourself, and when you first sit down at your desk to start your workday. And very important, practice in front of other people. Ask your spouse or colleague to listen to you and role-play a response.

At this point you might be thinking, "What happened to the 'minimum effective dose' theory?" Practice is where the rubber hits the road. If you want to be great, you will have to act like it. The minimum amount of effort required for greatness still requires significant work on your part. To keep practice manageable, I suggest using the triangle of successful preparation: every day for three days, rehearse each script three times at three different times throughout the day.

The triangle of successful preparation is particularly effective for practicing big presentations. For example, if I am doing a large-group workshop on Friday, I begin my script rehearsal on Tuesday. Right when I wake up, I take about five minutes and rehearse the scripted portions of my presentation three times. Then around lunch time I rehearse again, three times. Last thing at night, I rehearse again, three times. That's Day 1. Wednesday is Day 2, and I follow the same pattern. Thursday, Day 3, I repeat the three times three. On Friday, I make it a point before the presentation to go over the script at least three more times.

Don't worry that the practice will make you sound like a robot. When I asked Steve to rehearse, the first few runs did sound canned. I asked him to read through it a few times until he could remember his script by heart. Once he had it memorized, he started to sound more natural, authentic, and passionate. He was hooked. The next time I saw him, he told me that he didn't feel robotic at all, and he liked the process so much that he had written and practiced two additional scripts for other situations. He reported that his confidence on the phone was growing daily. Within a few weeks, he was building relationships and growing his business again.

There will be times when you have to prepare as if Coach Lombardi is standing over you screaming like a drill sergeant. Executives who have to enact large-scale layoffs often script and rehearse the words they will use with each individual employee; they write and practice the original notice as well as responses to common reactions. During the intense periods, they will work on their scripts for hours at a time, often practicing with executive colleagues or with outplacement or HR consultants. There will be times in your life when you face similar intense situations—either because forces outside of your control throw wrenches in your path, or because you are particularly driven to win. Step up to the plate at these critical yet temporary times; if you don't, you may struggle consistently. You choose: you can sacrifice when necessary, or you can suffer indefinitely.

Focus Through Confidence

Knowing what you will say and having it memorized and practiced builds confidence. You will be less distracted and stressed, thus producing a much improved level of focus. Having your confidence high greatly improves your ability to control your ideal arousal state (IAS). Having your fundamentally sound script coupled with your IAS allows you to communicate with great precision and passion, which lets you consistently outperform the competition.

If you want to perform like a champion, you have to prepare like one. Look at your business performance the same way many of the top athletes in the world look at theirs. Coach Lombardi's Green Bay Packers never ran a play they had not practiced to perfection. Athletes develop physical scripts; you will develop verbal scripts. There is no better way to develop performance-driving focus than planning and practicing exactly what you will say in the interactions most directly related to your success. Take the time to have your top three performance tasks scripted prior to performing, and use the triangle of success to prepare for those performances. As new performance tasks arise, create new scripts. Prepare and practice scripts, and watch your successes grow just as did Al Granum's on his way from the poorhouse to the penthouse.

Choose to Be Great

Mental Toughness Fundamental #7: Know Your Scripts. *Develop your focus by knowing and practicing what you are going to say . . . before you say it!*

Take the time to complete the following three tasks:

1. Mentally rehearse your most important script in your head once from beginning to end.
2. Looking into a mirror, practice out loud your most important script from beginning to end.
3. Teach a friend or colleague to make one script for success, and then allow that person to practice saying it in front of you.

CHAPTER 8

The Mental Workout

100 Seconds a Day Keeps Failure Away

John Ertz is the kind of man you would want to have teaching or coaching your children. Soft-spoken, he exudes both profound intelligence and charisma. He is confident, positive, and polite, and when he speaks he has already thought out the best way to say what he intends you to hear. Simply put, John Ertz is a great man, but he is neither a teacher nor a coach in the traditional sense of the word. John is one of the most successful managing partners at the insurance and investment giant Northwestern Mutual, and he is also a loving husband and terrific father. John has achieved that rare, magical combination of a highly successful professional life and a similar level of accomplishment in his personal life.

Over the years John has mentored thousands of businessmen and businesswomen. One of John's greatest leadership skills is that he wholeheartedly believes in his team members. Brett Wagner, John's training operations manager, states, "John is able to see things in people that they can't see themselves. When I started working for him, I was a mess, but he stuck with me. He gave me guidance, but he also let me find my own way. John is one of those great leaders who works with you in such a way that you just can't help but start believing in yourself."

Step into John's office, and you'll see evidence of all the awards he has received, as well as signed photographs of himself with dignitaries he has positively affected in one way or another. You'll find shelf after shelf of books about greatness: the classic *Good to Great* to the latest *10-Minute Toughness* (by yours truly) that John has read and studied to improve himself and his company. Yet you'll also notice picture after picture that shows John's personal side: photos of intimate embraces with his family, simple artwork by his kids when they were young, and even the following composition his daughter wrote in fifth grade:

> *My saint among us is John, and he is my dad. He is a saint at work, home, and at play. . . . His hard work makes it so we have a nice home, do fun activities, get a great education, and pay our bills. . . . Dad is really helpful. He helps me do my homework and quizzes me on my tests.*
>
> *He offers me guidance when I have problems. He has always helped me learn right from wrong. . . .*
>
> *He makes me feel better when I'm sad, and he always calls me when he's on his business trips. He reads next to me at night, before I go to bed. I know he loves me a lot. . . .*
>
> *Even when he gets mad, he talks nice. . . . My dad is a saint. He works hard at his job, home, and at play. He is very helpful, loving, patient, and kind. I love him very much, and I'm really lucky to have a dad like him.*

John Ertz wasn't born a great dad or an investment advisor. Instead, he *works* at achieving excellence every day. Even John will tell you that "just knowing your purpose and priorities in life isn't enough. You need to work at getting them into your DNA." A big part of his work involves dedication to mental toughness fundamental #8: prepare mentally every day.

PREPARE MENTALLY EVERY DAY: Complete a 100-second mental workout every day to dramatically improve your focus and ability to execute consistently.

John begins each day with a five-step mental workout to remind himself of exactly where he is trying to go in life and specifically what it will take from him that day to get there.

I developed the mental workout when I first began my work with professional athletes and realized very quickly it could be used successfully with business-minded individuals as well. The mental workout encapsulates only the most effective tools from the world of sport psychology and substantially improves attention and concentration; it really does take just 100 seconds to complete. Consistently completing the mental workout prior to the beginning of each workday trains your mind to (1) *stay positive*, (2) *focus* more efficiently, and (3) *execute* the key points of performance. Put simply, mentally rehearsing the specifics of where you are going and what it takes to get there will greatly enhance the likelihood of you achieving the success you want.

What Works for Olympians Will Work for You

To understand the power of the mental workout, consider the story of Justin Spring, one of the most decorated U.S. male gymnasts ever. With two events down at the 2007 National Championship, Justin tore his anterior cruciate ligament (ACL) on the landing of an otherwise perfect vault. He did not finish the meet; thus he did not qualify for the 2007 World Championships. But what scared him most was the fact that the 2008 Olympic Games were only 10 months away.

"My doctors told me it would take a year to get my knee back to 100 percent, but I knew I could make it happen. In the two years before, I had been through two ankle surgeries and a shoulder surgery, so I knew I could do it," he recalls. As soon as the swelling in his knee dissipated, Justin was under the knife. After a few months of rehab, it seemed as though everything was going well. But as he pushed himself to get back for the Olympics, Justin went too hard, too fast and ended up with patellar tendinitis. By January 2008, his Olympic dreams seemed a long shot at best. For the first time in his career, Justin lost the passion for the sport he had fallen in love with as a boy.

As part of a last-ditch effort to reignite his hope of competing in the Olympics, Justin and his coaches reached out to me for help. Justin began completing mental workouts in which he would focus his mind on completing his rehab and training with purpose and passion. "I was skeptical that I could get myself fired up about working out again, but I knew I had to do something. The mental workout helped me realize I had been just going through the motions. It reminded me again of the 'why' behind my effort." As part of the mental workout, Justin began visualizing his leg getting stronger. He also focused on what it would feel like to compete and win a medal in the Games. As he puts it, his "switch went on again." He started to believe in himself again and in what he could accomplish. He immediately started improving physically and mentally, and his Olympic-level confidence returned.

By June 2008, with a strong mind and knee, he competed at the Olympic trials for one of six spots on the team bound for Beijing. "By the trials, I had my mind so focused and ready, I knew I was going to make the team and win a medal in the Games. I had focused on it in my mental workouts so much that it had become my reality," remembers Justin. He did indeed make the team, which was at best predicted to finish no higher than eighth place. Justin disagreed: "Going into finals, my mind-set was, we are doing this! I had been through too much to that point not to finish what I had started."

"If you watch the coverage, you can actually see, right before I competed high bar, I was standing looking at the mat going through my mental workout. I was visualizing myself nailing the routine, and I was telling myself I was an Olympic medalist." With 1.3 billion viewers watching, Justin Spring rocked an almost perfect high bar set that propelled Team USA into an improbable bronze medal finish. "The truth is that I probably wouldn't even have been in the Olympics without the mental workouts, but now I can look in the mirror every day knowing I have accomplished *one* of my dreams," Justin says with a sparkle in his eye.

The mental workout works every bit as well, if not better, in business as it does in sports. At the highest level in athletics, one must be supremely talented to even have a chance at success. But in business, if you are physically fit (generally speaking) and mentally prepared, you are poised for great success. Think about it: when you make a sales call or give a performance review, it's not as if your toughest competitor is there on the mat with you trying to outsell you or snag your star contributor. And in business it isn't very likely you will blow your knee from here to kingdom come if you are just a bit short of perfect. Accountability, focus, and optimism alone—the three components of mental toughness—are enough to ensure high-level success in the corporate arena.

The Three Tools of the Five-Step Mental Workout

Your mind can be strengthened just like a muscle. The mental workout is a concrete and proven process that delivers results in the same way as a physical strengthening plan. That is, if you complete the exercises as instructed on a regular basis, you cannot help but become more mentally tough. Let's take a look at John Ertz's routine to identify the five steps of the mental workout, and then let's explore the details of each of the three concrete tools it incorporates.

JOHN ERTZ'S FIVE-STEP MENTAL WORKOUT	
Step 1: Centering Breath	John takes a deep centering breath to get calm and focused.
Step 2: Identity Statement	John says his identity statement to himself. It gives him the needed focus and confidence to attack each day.
Step 3: Vision and Integrity Highlight Reel	As he runs through his vision of self-image mental video, he pays particular attention to how great it will feel in five years to have accomplished the career and family goals he has set for himself. John uses the integrity visualization to rehearse and mentally imagine the highlights of the upcoming day. He zeroes in on his important client and staff meetings, as well as on being present each night at home with his beautiful wife and children. John visualizes how he wants to feel, what he wants to do, and how he wants things to turn out before they actually happen.
Step 4: Identity Statement	He repeats his identity statement to himself to drive home who he wants to be and how he wants his life to turn out.
Step 5: Centering Breath	John then takes another centering breath to remind him of the feeling of controlling his ideal arousal state (IAS), so he can return to this state throughout the day.

The Centering Breath

Pressure is everywhere in the business world. Whether you are preparing to make a sale, speak in front of the board, or interview a prospective job candidate, you feel the pressure associated with performance. From a scientific standpoint, the first physical response to pressure is the acceleration of your heart rate. The result: a tendency to rush the task at hand. That's why people tend to talk faster when they are nervous. Typically, rushing has a negative impact on performance. The more elevated the heart rate, the less likely the brain will remain at an optimal level of functioning. Trying to perform at a high level with your heart rate racing is like trying to perform intricate surgery in an ambulance barreling down a bumpy road. It's usually, if not always, a losing and frustrating proposition.

A very effective way to control heart rate is a centering breath. A purposeful, deep breath allows you to keep your heart rate under control so you will slow down and perform at a more effective pace. Centering breaths teach you to physiologically control your heart rate and better deal with pressure.

Take a moment now to practice a centering breath.

1. Breath in for six seconds.
2. Hold for two seconds.
3. Exhale for seven seconds.
4. Use a stopwatch to develop this rhythm; otherwise, you are likely to rush.

As you take this centering breath, you will feel the control set in. Feels good, doesn't it? When you use a centering breath at the start and end of your mental workout, you bring your heart rate under control and move into your IAS. In that place, your mind can settle into its most optimal performance level as you visualize and mentally rehearse what you are trying to accomplish and what it will take to get there.

Identity Statement

The identity statement is a self-description designed to improve how you see yourself in relation to your vision. It encapsulates your self-image, and it should be tailored to the type of person you hope to become. Remember from Chapter 2 that you will neither outperform nor underperform your self-image for long, so it's important to develop a self-image that is aligned with what you want to accomplish in life. That's why your identity statement includes your greatest strength and your greatest desire or desires, as expressed in your life priorities. When you say it to yourself, you begin to believe it. Consistently suggesting to yourself that you are a great success increases the likelihood of high self-image and accomplishment. In that way, through recitation of your identity statement you begin to create your new reality.

Written in the present tense, an identity statement begins with the affirmative "I am" and includes positive adjectives that describe the characteristics of the person you want and need to be to achieve your goals. It should also include a reference to your product goals as already having been achieved. Steve's identity statement reads:

I am happy and healthy. I am experiencing excellence in my career, and I am a great husband and father.

John Ertz's identity statement reads:

I am present and experience significance in my relationships. I live each day with heart and passion, and I am a leader in the company.

Some examples from other clients of mine:

I am confident and passionate about my work. I am the most creative marketing executive in the country.

I am full of positive energy, I make one million dollars per year, and I am an awesome mother and wife.

To create your identity statement, think about how successful you want to become in each of your priority areas. Describe that success succinctly here:

Priority 1: _____

Priority 2: _____

Priority 3: _____

Next, identify one or two personal characteristics you need to achieve what you desire.

Characteristic(s): _____

Now put it together in an "I am" statement that reflects your *future* ability to accomplish your dreams. You can come up with your own format, or use this template that reflects the previous examples:

I am [characteristic(s)]. I am [descriptors of success in each priority].

Identity Statement:

I am _____

_____

_____

Ten years ago, I was quite skeptical about the power of self-image and identity statements, but the more I tested the concepts with my clients, the more I realized the research was rock solid. I simply cannot tell you how often the creation and repetition of a strong identity statement has been *the* turning point that puts clients firmly on the road to success. Take, for example, Samantha, the owner of a small advertising agency, who set a product goal of personally netting one million from her operation. Although she progressed in many areas, she did not start making big money until she changed her identity statement from:

> *I am confident and creative; I am a highly successful businesswoman.*

to

> *I am confident and creative, and I personally make more than a million dollars a year.*

"Somewhere along the way, I began believing it was true," Sam says thoughtfully. If you ask her what changed, she will report that she really hadn't believed she could make more than a million dollars per year until she began repeating her identity statement daily.

When you truly believe in your ability to accomplish your goals, your corresponding self-image will motivate the behaviors you need to live up to your expectations. Your identity statement essentially becomes your personal mantra—a mantra that confirms you *are* the type of person who is successful and gets things done. Repeating your identity statement twice in each of your mental workouts actually locks in your propensity to achieve at the highest level. It builds your confidence and focuses your mind on achievement rather than on failure or excuses.

Vision and Integrity Highlight Reel

Your vision and integrity highlight reel consists of approximately 60 seconds of visualizing. You spend the first 30 seconds watching the vision of self-image mental video (created in Chapter 2) as a very detailed visualization of who and how you want to be 5 to 10 years in the future. Then you dedicate another 30 seconds to mentally rehearsing the important parts of your upcoming day so you can see what you need to do, and can do, in the next 24 hours to turn that vision into your new reality.

I call this second clip the integrity video because it helps you behave in a way that is aligned with your purpose, priorities, and goals. It acts like a mental script for your upcoming performance. Jack Nicklaus, quite possibly the greatest golfer of all time, explains his visualization work in the following way:

> I never hit a shot, not even in practice, without having a very sharp, in focus picture of it in my head. It's like a color movie. First I see the ball where I want it to finish, nice and white and sitting up high on bright green grass. Then the scene quickly changes, and I see the ball going there: its path, trajectory, and shape, and even its behavior on landing.[1]

Visualizing trains your mind to stay focused on your control points. To best develop that focus, visualize in first person, feel the emotions associated with success, and run the reels in actual time.

Guideline 1: Use the first-person vantage point. Visualizing from the first-person vantage point means looking at the video through your own eyes, so you see the things you would actually see while performing the task or skill. If you know you have a sales meeting with a client over lunch, then create an integrity video of exactly what you would see, say, and feel while sitting in your lunch seat looking across the table at your client. Visualizing from first person will help make the mental image a three-dimensional experience that feels real enough to increase your confidence and skill most efficiently.

Guideline 2: Emotionally feel the way you want to feel. The video you play in your head needs to capture the emotional experience you want to have. Why? Because through visualization, you create your reality, and reality involves emotions. When you allow negative emotions such as anger, embarrassment, or doubt to creep into your performances, you will not deliver the performance you need to succeed. One way to banish these emotions is to consciously replace them with productive, positive emotions during visualization.

As you visualize yourself in action, bring forth the emotions you want to feel during the tasks you are visualizing. Specifically feeling your IAS while visualizing relevant tasks will help produce the desired emotional states and increase your ability to consistently perform well. If you know you need to feel calm and confident as you begin the presentation you are visualizing, evoke a calm, confident feeling as you play your mental video. Need to feel courage and pride to make a cold call? Feel those emotions as you visualize yourself in that situation. Know that happiness is central to your relationship with your spouse? As you visualize your quality time with him or her, feel happiness. Visualization is a positive way to train yourself to have your desired emotions in place for performance.

Guideline 3: Visualize in actual time. Make sure to watch your mental clip in real speed, or the speed you want your performance to be. The idea is to create an image of *all* components of the performance, and speed is definitely a key component of any performance that involves speaking, attention to detail, sensing another's reactions, or demonstrating a full mastery of a topic. Rush through any performance that necessitates any of those activities, and you will struggle. If because of an increased heart rate, feelings of pressure or stress, or just plain busy-ness, you rush through your visualization, you will be teaching yourself to rush through the upcoming performance. Likewise, if you visualize in slow motion, you may teach yourself to go so slowly that you lose your audience or client's attention or come off as uncertain, unprepared, or unintelligent.

You may be wondering how you can visualize, for example, the delivery of an 80-second script, 3-minute sales call, or 30-minute presentation at real speed if you have only a 30-second block within your mental workout. That's a good question. You'll need to pick the most important specific moments within those events (5 to 10 seconds each) to run through in your visualization clips. Many people visualize in generalities not knowing that it is far less effective than visualizing the details. The key is to visualize specific moments of success that will serve your overall success.

Committing to Your Mental Workouts

Your mental workout is the most comprehensive way to train your mind to focus and maintain attention on the details of what causes success in your life. Just as your body responds to *consistent* strength training, your mind responds to *regular* mental workouts. Try to take the 100 seconds *each day* to develop your mental strength and stay in shape for performance. If you should miss a day here or there, don't panic. One missed appointment with your physical trainer won't sink your overall physical fitness, and the occasional missed mental workout won't kill your progression to success. If you do miss a day, simply make the commitment to get back on track the following day.

The Mental Workout

Step 1: Centering breath (15 seconds): Breathe in for 6 seconds. Hold for 2 seconds. Breathe out for 7 seconds.

Step 2: Identity statement (5 seconds): Recite your identity statement in your head.

Step 3: Vision and integrity highlight reel (60 seconds): Run in your head your vision of self-image video and then your integrity video clip:

- Your vision of self-image, as developed in Chapter 2
- Your integrity video in which you visualize yourself doing the tasks you need to do within the next day to make your vision of self-image become a reality

Step 4: Identity statement (5 seconds): Repeat your identity statement to yourself.

Step 5: Centering breath (15 seconds): Breathe in for 6 seconds. Hold for 2 seconds. Breathe out for 7 seconds. Know that your mind is focused and ready to perform.

In Chapter 2, I asked you to calendar in 30 seconds to review your vision of self-image. Now that you have instructions for all of the steps of the mental workout, you can take that 30-second commitment out of your calendar and replace it with the full 100-second version. Precisely when during your day you complete the mental workout is up to you. Many prefer to pin it to activities they do every day: going to bed at night or waking up in the morning. Research suggests that visualization right before sleep integrates the visions into dreams and therefore raises the effectiveness of the visualization. Others have found that the best results are achieved when the workout is completed within a few minutes of waking up, when the mind is clear and uncluttered.[2] However, many of my business clients prefer to complete the mental workout at the start of the workday, just before things really get rolling, so that they are fully ready for what lies ahead.

I find it very hard to believe that anyone is so busy that he or she can't find 100 seconds—1 minute and 40 seconds—to undertake the single most important step toward effectively executing those tasks most linked to success. One hundred seconds is about the same time it takes to dry off after a shower or delete the junk mail from your inbox. I've seen that failure to complete the mental workout isn't necessarily a matter of lack of time as much as it is a function of lack of habit. Even though you may rationally agree that it's a great way to use 1 minute and 40 seconds of your time, you may forget to do it on a regular basis. So do what you need to do to lock it in as a new habit:

> Prioritize mental workout completion by taking a moment right now to decide exactly when and where completing the mental workouts will fit into your schedule. Then take the time to reserve that time daily in your electronic or paper calendar.

By making mental workouts a habit, you will set yourself on a trajectory toward developing mental toughness and focus as you have never experienced. By spending no more than 15 minutes a week on these workouts, you will experience *dramatic* and *immediate* improvements in your ability to achieve personal and professional success.

Choose to Be Great

Mental Toughness Fundamental #8: Prepare Mentally Every Day. *Complete a 100-second mental workout every day to dramatically improve your focus and ability to execute consistently.*
Take the time to complete the following three tasks:

1. Using the guidelines for the mental workout, practice your mental workout from beginning to end one time.
2. Commit to starting your regular mental workouts tomorrow.
3. Within the next 24 hours, teach a colleague or friend the five-step mental workout.

DEVELOPING EXECUTIVE TOUGHNESS CHARACTERISTIC 3

Optimism:
Overcoming All Obstacles

9

Relentless Solution Focus

The Ultimate Measure of Mental Toughness

J ack Canfield refuses to give up or give in. You may even call him *relentless*. In the fall of 1991, Jack had just cowritten a book. Unfortunately, every major publishing house he met with told him that "short stories don't sell." After the compilation was rejected by more than 30 publishers, Jack's agent apologized and suggested that he give up trying to get a book contract.

Undeterred, Jack relentlessly focused on the next possible solution. He created "pledge to buy" forms that he had friends, family, and attendees of his speeches sign. He then jetted off to Anaheim, California, to the American Booksellers Association convention. Armed with pledges promising sales of more than 20,000 copies, he doggedly went from booth to booth. After being rejected by another 130 publishers, Jack finally stumbled on Health Communications, Inc., a struggling outfit specializing in addiction-and-recovery books. Jack somehow convinced the copresidents, Peter Vegso and Gary Seidler, to look at the manuscript. Within a few weeks, Jack and his coauthor, Mark Victor Hansen, finally had a deal.

But once published, the book didn't sell at the level Jack had hoped. Again Jack was relentless. His solution was *the rule of five*: do five things every day to move sales of the book in the right direction. He would do five radio interviews, send five copies to review editors, or reach out to five marketing firms in the hope that they may recommend the book to their clients.

Jack called talk shows and spoke with anyone he could think of, from military personnel to gas station attendants. He even sent copies to all the jurors in the O. J. Simpson case in hopes that a camera might catch a snapshot of the book for the world to see. For two years Jack committed himself to completing five sales-driving tactics every day. Finally, the book caught on to such an extent that you're sure to recognize its title: *Chicken Soup for the Soul*. Because of all of Jack's effort, his book has sold more than eight million copies and has been translated into 39 languages worldwide.

What sets individuals like Jack Canfield apart from the pack is a quality I call relentless solution focus (RSF). In fact, mental toughness fundamental #9 is to develop a relentless solution focus.

DEVELOP A RELENTLESS SOLUTION FOCUS:
Within 60 seconds, replace all problem-focused thought with solution-focused thinking to dramatically improve your health, happiness, and success.

Whether you define winning as making more money, improving your personal relationships, or increasing your level of personal health and happiness, RSF will dramatically increase your chances of achieving that win. RSF exemplifies the third characteristic of mental toughness, optimism. Remember from the introduction of this book that we adopted the following definition for optimism:

> **OPTIMISM:** Hopefulness and confidence about the future or successful outcome of something; a tendency to take a favorable or hopeful view.

We saw how researchers like Dr. Martin Seligman have linked optimism to happiness, health, success, and longevity. It seems that optimism isn't just a core component of mental toughness; it may well also be *the* key to life. Optimistic people are simply sure that their lives will work out. With hope and confidence central to their thinking, their minds stay focused on solutions, especially in the face of adversity. That sounds a lot like my definition of mental toughness, which is essentially your ability to be optimistic that your life will turn out the way you want because of the effort you put into that mission.

The link between optimism and success comes down to expectancy theory: that which you focus on expands. Expectancy theory has proven over and over again that when people focus on problems, their problems actually grow and reproduce.

My professional findings indicate that not even 30 percent of the population in the United States describe themselves as content with their ability to achieve their life goals. It appears that it is normal to focus on problems and thereby create more problems. It makes you wonder if we are designed to be happy and successful, or miserable and underachieving.

But the great thing about expectancy theory is that there's another side of the coin. If indeed whatever people focus on expands, then people hold a huge opportunity within their brains. When you train your mind to focus on solutions, guess what expands? Solutions! When you use RSF to change your outlook, you become mentally tough and leave normal people behind in a world focused on problems.

PCT: Public Enemy #1

The number one reason mental toughness is so difficult is a tendency that I call problem-centric thought (PCT). PCT is the polar opposite of RSF. While RSF is rare, PCT is somewhat biologically inevitable. For whatever reason, our brains are built in a way that PCT comes more naturally than RSF. It's natural to focus on mistakes, the past, barriers, and what you don't have rather than on what you do have. It's easier to think about problems such as not having enough money or success than it is to acknowledge good fortune and abundance. Think of our relationship to oxygen, the most valuable resource known to humankind. Without it, we die quickly. But when is the last time you thought, "Wow, this is terrific! This is great! I have an abundance of the most important resource known to humankind!" We all have a tendency to take the positive for granted. We allow it to become the faint background for the problems we draw in intricate, larger-than-life detail.

To make matters even worse, our society reinforces our PCT tendency. Since we all share the propensity for PCT, we commonly relate to one another through PCT communication. If you watch the news, do you see more about problems or solutions? When you go to the normal 90-minute movie, how much time is spent on the problem as opposed to the solution? When people congregate around the watercooler, what are they most likely to discuss: problems and the past, or solutions and the future? And when you meet up with customers, are they more likely to talk about their problems or the solutions you've put on the table?

Clearly, we are all very good at thinking about and talking about our problems. We love to sit and think about them and feel sorry for ourselves. I'd go as far as to say that my professional colleagues in psychology reinforce the focus on problems. During my training, I was schooled in a widely popular communication technique called the ABCs of communication:

- A is *I feel . . .*
- B is *when you . . .*
- C is *in this situation.*

In the early days of my private practice, I dutifully taught couples in my counsel to use this format. It didn't take long to notice that the couples were leaving my office in worse shape than they came in. By asking them to use the ABCs, I was actually asking them to communicate with a problem focus. So I looked for empirical evidence supporting the success of the ABCs of communication. Guess what? There is none. In fact, I came to see that not only much of my traditional training but also how Americans are raised reinforces our need to talk about problems to find solutions. All of that is simply a myth. Expectancy theory, on the other hand, proves itself time and time again. Let me be clear in leaving much of modern clinical psychology practice behind: *Talking about your problems will lead to more problems, not to solutions.* If you want solutions, start thinking and talking about your *solutions.*

Easier said than done, I know. You will have to develop significant mental toughness to escape the PCT pull. The simple "don't be negative" pep talks we've all heard from parents and bosses do not offer enough substance to support this depth of change in thinking. What does help is (1) logically analyzing how PCT and RSF deliver vastly different outcomes, and (2) using concrete and proven tools to change how your mind thinks. Let's start with an example that highlights the results of PCT versus RSF.

A Day in the Life of PCT and RSF

Here's an example of how expectancy theory plays out in the life of a typical executive. A hospital administrator who happens to allow herself to have a PCT day enters a board meeting unaware that a multimillion-dollar lawsuit has been recently filed against her hospital. Upon hearing the news delivered by the already uptight and now angry president of the board, the PCT administrator becomes defensive and blames the board for not giving her the necessary resources to stay on top of priority matters such as potential lawsuits. The PCT administrator goes on to single out one board member, Sharon, in particular, for vetoing every budget proposal the PCT administrator had turned in. During the meeting, board members make it clear that they feel it is the hospital administrator's responsibility to be more on top of matters like the lawsuit.

After leaving the meeting, the PCT administrator heads to her office, all the while thinking to herself what a mistake it had been to have entered the morning board meeting unprepared. She had known for quite some time there was a potential malpractice suit, but she had felt there wasn't enough merit for the patient to actually go through with it. The PCT administrator then starts beating herself up for not having followed up more with the patient and wonders if that attention could have averted the mess she was now in. The PCT administrator also begins thinking about how she had singled out Sharon in the meeting. She knows Sharon carries a lot of weight with the board, and she fears that she is in great jeopardy of losing her job because of how she reacted defensively to the feedback at the meeting. As she enters her office, she closes the door and begins to pace back and forth as she broods over her mounting problems.

Pacing, the PCT administrator fails to realize the start time of the mandatory staff meeting she called has come and gone. Her phone rings, and her assistant informs her that the staff is gathered and becoming impatient. The PCT administrator remembers that she had been dreading this presentation about new budget cuts and how the hospital would need to operate more efficiently in the future to remain profitable. In her haste to get to the meeting, the PCT administrator grabs the wrong file.

Still distracted, the PCT administrator apologizes as she steps into the meeting room to begin her presentation. She opens her file and realizes she has the wrong notes. Instead of delaying the meeting any longer, she decides to proceed. After 15 minutes of trying her best to recall the specific protocol changes and implementation dates, the PCT administrator unsuccessfully attempts to answer questions. The staff grow agitated and make it clear that they will have their union reps continue the conversation with her.

On the long walk back to her office, the PCT administrator, with head down, shoulders slumped, and feeling absolutely miserable, replays in her mind the day's mounting tally of mistakes.

This has been a story of expectancy theory in action: *a focus on problems causes more problems.*

Now let's rewind and go through the same day with the RSF administrator. She enters the board meeting unaware that a multimillion-dollar lawsuit has been recently filed against the hospital. Upon hearing the news delivered by the already uptight and now angry president of the board, the RSF administrator feels herself immediately flip into defensive mode. Her mind begins to swirl, and she begins to think about how her budget has been cut practically in half over the last two years. She zeroes her thoughts in on Sharon, a board member who rejected every new budget proposal she had presented. But before saying anything, RSF administrator catches herself focusing on the problems. She makes the conscious decision to emphasize solutions instead.

The RSF administrator takes a deep breath and asks herself, "What is the number one thing I can do right now that could make this situation better?" She responds by letting the board know she will definitely work to do a better job in the future. She then refocuses the board on potential solutions: "What's done is done. I think what's most important at this point is for us to identify the absolute best way to proceed." This time, the board joins her in working up forward-thinking solutions. The RSF administrator agrees to be in touch with the hospital's lead attorney on the suit and also to create a team to head up improvements to the current hospital standards and protocols. After leaving the meeting, the RSF administrator heads to her office. She finds that her mind wants to focus on how big of a problem the pending lawsuit poses. Yet she forces her mind to focus on solutions by asking herself, "What is one thing I can do right now that could make things better?"

Forcing her mind to focus on moving forward, the RSF administrator reviews her calendar and is reminded that she has a staff meeting within the hour to go over the budget and associated changes. She decides that the best possible thing to do is to spend 15 minutes going over her notes and making any final adjustments to her presentation.

After reviewing and rehearsing the key points of her staff presentation, RSF administrator arrives a few minutes early to the staff meeting to double-check the audiovisual equipment. She then promptly begins the meeting, makes a concise and compelling presentation, and answers each and every staff question with compassion and confidence, at which point the staff breaks into working groups to take on tasks related to the proposed changes. Walking back to her office afterward, she again begins to fixate on how much of a problem the lawsuit will be, and she wonders about her own job stability. The RSF administrator catches herself focusing on problems and forces herself to ask and answer, yet again, the question, "What is one thing I can do differently that could make this better?" After thinking for a few minutes, she decides the best course of action would be to reach out by phone to the hospital's lead attorney to begin discussions about the lawsuit. She also decides to bring in a public relations specialist to discuss possible damage control.

This has been a story of expectancy theory in action: *focusing on solutions brings about more solutions.*

Have you made a mistake by saying the wrong thing to your spouse or to your boss, or by committing a blunder at work, and then allowed yourself to think about the mistake long after it was over? Of course you have, or you wouldn't be a human being. Have you ever dwelt on the past and crowded out thoughts of the future? We all do: remember PCT causes our brains to focus on problems. The great news is that you can learn to use RSF to focus on solutions and become optimistic. Let's turn to concrete tools you can use to make RSF your standard of operation.

Ultimately for you to develop mental toughness you will need to stop giving yourself permission to have thoughts or conversations that highlight your weaknesses, negativity, or obstacles to success. Always focus on your strengths and what you can do to improve and persevere. Don't be the one at the watercooler talking about how terrible management is or how underresourced your department is. Be that leader who identifies ways to improve management and increase potential resources. Replace complaining about the kids to your spouse with offering ideas to help make improvements to the children's behaviors. Make the commitment to *never* again be the complainer and to *always* take control of making your life and situation better.

The Tool to Be *Relentless*

Let's review the definition of RSF: within 60 seconds of having any negative or self-doubting thought, replace the negative thinking with solution-focused thought. Remember that it is abnormal to switch from PCT to RSF. In fact, optimism is abnormal. That is why if you can develop mental toughness, you will have an edge in your personal and professional life. Just as you would use actionable tools to differentiate your products or services, you should use a specific tool, in this case a simple question, to control your mind and switch to RSF. Anytime you catch yourself focusing on a problem, negativity, or self-doubt, ask yourself this question: *What is one thing I can do differently that could make this situation better?*

Asking and answering this question will undoubtedly develop your mental toughness. Your thoughts are the control panel for your feelings and behaviors. Therefore, the trick to controlling the way you feel and behave is learning to control your thoughts. Replacement thinking is a great way of seizing that control. We know that negative thoughts are going to come into our heads: that's PCT. I wish I had a tool for erasing negative thoughts altogether, but I haven't come up with one yet. Instead, focus on *replacing* every negative thought with a solution within 60 seconds. Your mind can *fully* focus on only one thing at a time, and if you are completely focused on a solution, you cannot be thinking about your problems. Your mind has only so much space, so what you put in will crowd out what's already there. Replacement thinking is the most effective way to get the negative garbage out of your head. If you ask and answer the RSF question each time your mind has zeroed in on a problem, you will shift your mind to more effective solution-focused thinking. You have 60 seconds to become aware of your negative thought, ask the question, and come up with an answer. Don't worry if your initial solution ends up being ineffective: the +1 solution concept described shortly will take care of that.

No one else can do the work for you to commit to RSF: not a spouse, not a friend, not a boss, not even the greatest corporate leader in the world. You alone are responsible for your thoughts, and you alone can control them. The CEO of a Fortune 35 told me that he used to try to lead by telling his people exactly what to do to overcome the problems they faced. He was surprised that his solutions, which worked quite well for him, didn't generate the same results when his subordinates tried to implement them. Curious, he experimented by removing himself as the expert. He resisted giving his people solutions. Instead, he asked them a question that is now familiar to you: what is one thing you can do to make this situation better? He then listened to their solutions and supported them as they tried them out. After tracking results for more than a year, he found not only that his people were coming up with solutions he hadn't thought of, but also that the solutions were actually working better than what he had been offering them.

The Mental Chalkboard

In the spirit of accountability, become accountable to yourself for using the RSF question. Imagine for a moment that you have a chalkboard in your head that looks like the following:

Problems	Solutions

What is one thing I can do differently that could make this better?

If I were to open up your head and look at your chalkboard, I would most likely see a completely filled-out problem side and in comparison, a somewhat blank solution side. Like everyone else, you need to learn to get from the problem side of the board to the solution side of the board. Every time you catch yourself on the problem side, you have to ask and answer the RSF question, what is one thing

I can do differently that could make this better? When you force yourself to ask and answer this question, you move to the solution side. Do that time and time again, and the balance of the board shifts completely.

Sometimes we get so caught up in life that we don't even realize we are living on the problem side of the board. How do you know if you are sitting on that left side? You're there anytime you feel negative emotions like anger, sadness, frustration, or fear. Let your negative emotions serve as your indicator lights that you need to ask and answer the RSF question and move from the problem side to the solution side.

+1 Solutions: One Step at a Time

The second you cross over the barrier to the solution side of your mental chalkboard, negative emotions will immediately stop increasing. They won't necessarily decrease; they just stop growing. That's a good thing. But ultimately, you want to get to a point where the negative emotions decrease. You'll get to that place only when you find a solution that sticks, one that you know will actually help you overcome the problem noted. To ensure you have the necessary perseverance to continue searching for the viable solution, you must first realize that each and every problem has a solution. There's *always* a +1 solution that brings you one step closer to a full solution.

+1 SOLUTION: *Any* improvement to the current situation.

Most people want a solution that produces complete resolution to the problem. That's like trying to climb a mountain with one step. You overcome problems one step at a time, one improvement at a time. Any improvement, small or large, is a solution: a +1 solution, to be precise. Think about stranded Nando Parrado making his way back to safety: each and every step he took to get off that mountain was just as valuable as the very last step he took in his journey. When you believe that every problem, no matter how large, has at the very least a +1 solution, you will find it easier to stay on the solution side of the chalkboard and banish negative thoughts.

Often you will think about a solution for a while and realize it's not going to work. The second you mentally cross your solution off, you go right back to the problem side of the board. If you allow yourself to stay there, your negative emotions will increase and your problem will get bigger. But if you are relentless about answering the RSF question, "What is one thing I can do differently that could make this better?" you'll return to the solution side. It is quite likely that several of the solutions you come up with won't work. After you fail a few times with finding a viable solution, you will want to tell yourself, "You know what, this problem just doesn't have a solution." If you tell yourself there is no solution to your problem, guess what? There isn't one and there won't be: expectancy theory is at work, expanding what you're focusing on.

You need to use a +1 solution to escape success-robbing, happiness-draining PCT, and you need to do so relentlessly. If your first solution doesn't work, try again. Remember this mental toughness fundamental isn't called solution focus, it's appropriately named *relentless* solution focus. Be relentless by asking and answering the RSF question, "What is one thing I can do differently that could make my situation better?" and find a +1 solution every time you catch yourself basking in problems. The key to optimism is to continue searching for the solution no matter how difficult it is to identify one that works.

Think about how many times Jack Canfield went back to the drawing board to find solutions before he achieved his goal. Think also about Rick Little. At 19 years old Rick decided he wanted to help high-school-age kids live more effective and fulfilling lives by learning to communicate, setting goals, and dealing better with conflict. For one year, Rick experienced absolutely nothing but rejection to his plan. He was living out of his car and eating peanut butter crackers to survive. Rick crossed a solution off 155 times.

Finally, he found one that stuck: the Kellogg Foundation agreed to give Rick $130,000 to launch his project. Rick continued to be relentless in his dream to help kids, and eventually he raised more than $100 million dollars to spread his Quest program to more than 30,000 schools and help millions of kids per year develop their ability to live happier and more successful lives.

If you want to be a success, you can never stop believing there is a solution. You must relentlessly keep searching for a solution, no matter whether you have crossed off 2 solutions or 200.

The fact is that every problem has a solution, if you use the +1 definition.

Assessing RSF—Expecting RSF

RSF is the single greatest gift you can give to yourself, your employees, and your children. By adopting the RSF mentality yourself, you will be a role model and show others how to personally take complete control of life. When a person feels a lack of control, PCT is inevitable. RSF guarantees that no matter how bad things are you can always do something to make it better. On a scale of 1 to 10, with 1 being "rarely focusing on solutions" to 10 being "always focusing on solutions," how relentless are you?

If, for instance, you replace negative thinking with solution-focused thought within 60 seconds 30 percent of the time, you would be a 3 on the RSF scale. Before learning about RSF, most people rate themselves a 4. Steve, whose story we've been following throughout this book, started at a 5 and after a few weeks of work consistently ranked himself at 9. With a commitment to the consistent application of the tools in this chapter, you, too, can expect to improve one number each week.

> Commit to a one-number-a-week progression on your RSF goal until you achieve a 9, and then commit to holding yourself there.

People fall short with RSF not because they don't believe in it but because they tend to get subconsciously sucked back into PCT. Keep RSF alive in your mind every day by completing the following tasks:

1. Set a phone reminder every day at 2:30 P.M. that says "RSF." (I chose this time because our biological mental clocks begin to wear down midafternoon, making us more susceptible to PCT.)
2. Add the RSF scale to your daily success logs (see Chapter 5), and give yourself an honest assessment every day.

You can find success log work sheets (with the RSF assessment question included) on my website http://www.jasonselk.com.

A consistent commitment to RSF guarantees to help you correct or improve the mental part of your performance. You'll become more optimistic, and therefore, you will enjoy life more and experience much greater levels of personal and professional achievement. Yes, some days you'll find it harder than others to keep your RSF. Go back to your tool, ask the RSF question, and relentlessly search until you find a viable +1 solution, and you will take control of each and every problem that life throws your way. You'll undoubtedly learn to face life's challenges with hope and confidence and, above all, results-producing optimism.

Choose to Be Great

Mental Toughness Fundamental #9: Develop a Relentless Solution Focus. *Within 60 seconds, replace all problem-focused thought with solution-focused thinking to dramatically improve your health, happiness, and success. Develop optimism by asking and answering the RSF question: "What is one thing I can do differently to make this better?"*

Take the time to complete the following three tasks:

1. Write the RSF question, "What is one thing I can do differently to make this situation better" on three note cards and tape one to your bathroom mirror, the dashboard of your car, and the corner of your desk to help strategically remind you to relentlessly focus on solutions.

2. Make the commitment in your next meeting at work to ask out loud the RSF question, "What is one thing we can do differently to make this situation better?" every time the dialogue begins to focus on problems. Count how many times you had to ask the question, and share the information with your colleagues.

3. Next time you hear a friend or family member focusing on problems, teach them how you use the RSF question to replace negativity with optimism.

CHAPTER 10

Gable Discipline

Optimism Through Unremitting Action

Dan Gable represents the epitome of discipline. Unique and intense even in his sixties, he speaks with an intensity that transmits the effort he puts into his thoughts. Gable has been the best in the world twice; undeniably the greatest wrestler the world has ever seen, Gable is also known as the best college wrestling coach in history. His approach to achieving his spectacular success is quite straightforward: develop a plan and then have the discipline to execute the plan, and if that doesn't work, become more disciplined.

In 1970, following a high school wrestling career in which he was undefeated, Dan Gable sat perched atop college wrestling, poised for perfection again, with 118 wins and no losses. Dale Bahr, one of Gable's teammates, commented about Gable's discipline-driven four years at Iowa State University.

> Quite frankly, when he came in as a freshman, he wasn't that good . . . I used to beat on him in practice. He couldn't get away from me. But he kept working and working and working, and when one guy would get

tired, stop, get a drink, and come back, Gable would be working with another guy. And if that guy got tired or maybe hurt or something, Dan wouldn't stop and wait for him to go get taped, he'd just go get somebody else. In the course of a practice he'd wear out two, three, four of his teammates.[1]

Up to the point of his last college wrestling match, Dan Gable was already considered to be one of the greatest American wrestlers of all time and his future seemed to promise more of the same. The prospect of going undefeated for an entire college career was so compelling that in the run-up to the last match, ABC's "Wide World of Sports" chronicled Gable's quest for perfection and planned to cover the presumed historic event in its entirety. Usually, Gable allowed nothing to get in the way of his mental and physical preparation. But fortunately for his opponent, Larry Owings, Gable entered his last collegiate match without the discipline that had previously protected him from defeat. "I am usually so disciplined, but I definitely lost my focus that day. I knew I should have been thinking about myself and what I needed to do, but instead I was focused on Owings and the thrill of it all. 'Wide World of Sports' convinced me to do an interview an hour before the match. I knew I shouldn't have," recalls Gable. With distractions and without his characteristic mental discipline, Gable lost the last match of his epic collegiate career.

Using the loss for motivation, a post-college Gable became as unstoppable as a freight train on the wrestling mat. As Gable prepared for the upcoming 1972 Olympic Games, his legend grew to a point where the Russian Federation of Athletes set a goal to beat Gable. Note that it wasn't merely the wrestling program, but the *entire* Russian Federation that had its Cold War–era eyes set on him. Under this pressure, Gable won the gold medal without having a single point scored on him. In reflecting on his career, Gable said, "The bottom line is that losing the Owings match helped me. I needed to get beat. Because it not only helped me win the Olympics, but it helped me *dominate* the Olympics . . . I would have a hundred times rather not have lost, but I used it. I used it."[2]

A month after the Olympics, Gable became the first assistant wrestling coach at the University of Iowa. Within a few years Gable was promoted to the head coach role of the program that would eventually become the perennial powerhouse of the sport. From the beginning of his coaching career, he instilled in his wrestlers the importance of discipline. He didn't, and still doesn't, cut corners. He motivated his athletes to push beyond their limits in practice, and he was equally as relentless in making sure they put energy into proper recovery and mental preparation. As a coach, Gable would go on to win nine straight NCAA championships and a total of fifteen in a 21-year stretch.

Randy Lewis, one of Gable's wrestlers who won the Olympic gold in 1984, once told me the following story about returning to his alma mater later in his successful career:

> I was 31 years old, and in the previous two months I had just beaten the top three ranked wrestlers in the world. I then wrestled Gable, who was 41 at the time, and he beat me 15–5. He completely dominated me. Gable is probably the most disciplined person to walk the face of the earth, and the discipline he taught me is the reason I've had success.

I have had the great pleasure of knowing Coach Gable for over twenty years, and in a recent conversation he told me that discipline is a big piece of mental toughness:

> You need to know what your issues are, and you need to work on them until they become strengths. If there is

hesitation, it means you're not ready and that you need help. In those cases, you may need to find someone or something that helps you get better. Either way, you need to find a way to get it done.

Intrinsically inspired by this great hero, mentor, and role model, mental toughness fundamental #10 is to adopt Gable discipline.

ADOPT GABLE DISCIPLINE: When you set your mind to do something, find a way to get it done . . . no matter what!

While relentless solution focus (RSF) represents the *mental* step of optimism, discipline is the *action* step that makes solutions materialize. True optimism comes from knowing without a doubt that you can create the outcome you desire. Your confidence comes from the secure knowledge that you will indeed follow through on doing what it takes to succeed. Coach Gable made sure to emphasize to me that doing whatever it takes should never include doing anything illegal, immoral, or unethical. With proper discipline, there is always a way to succeed within the rules. Gable didn't push himself and then his athletes because he *wondered* if he or they could achieve positive outcomes: he pushed because he *knew* he and his athletes would succeed. That absolute knowledge is the ultimate expression of the hope and confidence that characterize optimism.

While some people mistakenly associate optimism with the vague belief that divine intervention or some other outside force will make good things happen, those who are mentally tough know that their own accountability, focus, and hard work cause positive outcomes. In other words, optimistic people know they control their own lives because they tirelessly translate hope and confidence into success through disciplined action.

In this way, discipline delivers success. Discipline applies to all aspects of mental toughness, from following through on articulating and refining your life purpose and priorities, to setting and evaluating goals, to focusing on the tasks that deliver leadership performance and drive the achievement of your win. Without following through on any aspect of the plan, you jeopardize your success. That's why developing discipline is the last, and most essential, mental toughness fundamental.

Gable Discipline

For several years, I tried to emphasize the importance of discipline to my clients simply by telling them that it was important that they follow through. Time and time again, they would come back and report that they hadn't been finishing their daily process goals, completing their mental workouts, or developing an RSF. I determined that it was up to me to find a way to make the idea of discipline more "sticky." I started referring to *Gable* discipline. I told my clients the story of how I became personally acquainted with this legend and his philosophy:

In 1990, a friend of mine who at the time was one of Coach Gable's University of Iowa wrestlers invited me to watch practice. Boy, did this coach push his athletes, especially at the end of practice. He told them to pump up the intensity for the last 5 minutes, but then he kept them fighting at national-competition intensity for another 15.

After practice, the coach and the team retired to a sweltering 190-degree Fahrenheit sauna, and I joined them. I studied Coach Gable. He sat rocking back and forth, watching sweat drip from the extended pinkies of his clasped hands. His focus and pent-up energy reminded me of a caged animal. One by one, his highly conditioned athletes took refuge outside the sauna. I gave up, too. Yet he remained, staring at the sweat dripping from his pinkies. He later told me that he had set a goal of counting 500 drips of sweat. He simply refused to leave the heat until he had achieved his goal. He taught me that "with practice, self-discipline becomes a habit." Intrigued and inspired, I thought of Coach Gable and his discipline daily.

Invoking the rule of three, I also laid out for my clients the core components of Gable discipline:

1. **Prioritize discipline:** Discipline or self-control is a limited resource. Be sure to choose wisely where you will use your self-restraint. For you to be successful in business, you will need to develop and use your discipline on those tasks that are most necessary for your success: your process goals.
2. **Finish what you start:** Discipline your mind to focus on getting started on your commitments and then use discipline to finish these tasks completely. Each time you follow through with a commitment, you reinforce your ability to finish the next time.
3. **Try, try again:** If you come up short on your discipline, keep fighting, kicking, and scratching to improve. Find the nearest mirror and look yourself in the eye while you tell yourself, "There is no excuse, and this will not happen again." Get outside help if needed, but never, ever give up on being disciplined.

With this inspiration and outline, clients began following through more consistently. They would call or e-mail me or come into my office and tell me that Gable discipline had worked, or that they were just about to give up when they thought of Coach Gable counting every drop of sweat until he reached his goal. The message about the importance of discipline had stuck.

Take a moment right now and assess your level of discipline.

On a 1 to 10 scale, using a realistic evaluation, how well do you follow through with all the things you tell yourself you need to do?

1   2   3   4   5   6   7   8   9   10

If you are a 10, you have already developed Gable discipline and you are probably experiencing great success.

If you are any number less than a 10, even if you are a 9, work on improving your discipline by using the tips in this chapter.

When it comes to discipline, 90 percent isn't good enough. You need to go all the way like Coach Gable. Otherwise you open the door for falling short on following through with your most important tasks, and you thereby risk your achievement of success.

Making Discipline a Habit

Tools work only when you have the discipline to use them. Yet we have all witnessed just how fleeting discipline can be. If you have ever tried to hold yourself back from having that last piece of pizza, to put down the cigarette for good, or to hold your temper when subordinates make mistakes, you know just how difficult it is to maintain the discipline needed to become the person you hope to be.

Yet without discipline, you are in trouble. Specifically, without a profound commitment to Gable discipline, you simply will not perform at a leadership level or achieve your win. The good news is that you can learn to make Gable discipline a habit that over time will come more and more naturally to you. You can turn fleeting or normal discipline into lifelong Gable discipline by limiting temptation, "over-practicing" discipline, and teaming up with a mental coach.

Limit Temptation

Being disciplined can be exhausting. The more often you put yourself in a position to need discipline, the harder it will be to maintain it. Remember that self-control is a limited resource. You have only so much discipline within you, so you want to spend it on what is most important. With your process goals, you have a list of your most important priorities. Limit the temptations in your life so you don't have to use so much of your reserve of discipline to get these priorities done.

Let's use Steve again as an example. Steve knows it is imperative that he get his 20 dials, 3 meetings, and 90 minutes of organization in each day. That adds up daily to an eight-hour workload. Steve completes his most important process goals early in the day and limits his temptations by asking his assistant to address all e-mail and phone calls that come in throughout the day. At 4:30 each afternoon, she presents Steve with a list of all the phone calls and e-mails he needs to respond to personally. He then spends half an hour handling these "distractions," knowing that his career process goals are already complete for the day.

Steve also knows that he needs to prioritize time each day with his wife and kids. To limit temptation, he refuses to stop on the way for a drink with colleagues. That way, he won't have to tap into his discipline reserves to leave after having "just one." Upon arriving home, Steve avoids turning the television on; he's very aware just how much discipline he would need to stop watching his favorite program halfway through.

You will be better at maintaining the discipline needed for your high-level success if you avoid some temptations altogether. If you know you have a weakness for "surfing the

Net," then don't allow yourself to go online. If you have difficulty saying, "I can't talk now, I'm working" to friends who call you during the day, avoid answering the phone during the workday. Achieving your win will require sacrifice. Make it easier for yourself by avoiding those temptations that force you to spend some of your discipline reserves.

> List one temptation you can do a better job of avoiding for each of your three priority areas:
>
> I will work on avoiding the following temptation that will help me improve in my priority 1:
>
> _____
>
> I will work on avoiding the following temptation that will help me improve in my priority 2:
>
> _____
>
> I will work on avoiding the following temptation that will help me improve in my priority 3:
>
> _____

"Over-Practice" Discipline

Because discipline is a skill, you can improve it through conscious practice. Just as baseball players practice swinging with a weighted bat so that in a game they feel an advantage and improve their batting average, you can improve your discipline by pushing yourself further in your conscious practice of discipline. I call this technique over-practicing discipline.

One way to over-practice discipline is to choose one process goal to overachieve one time per week. For example, every Friday Steve chooses one of his process goals and does just a little more than what he generally expects of himself. He may make 22 dials (instead of stopping at 20), or he may spend 40 minutes on his stationary bike as opposed to his normal 30. Steve chooses Friday to over-practice his discipline because he knows it is one of the hardest days for him to stay committed. Working at a higher intensity on Fridays reinforces Steve's ability to maintain discipline on the other days of the week.

> Take a moment and mentally decide which day of the week you will over-practice discipline by overshooting at least one of your process goals.
> You may want to consider placing an appointment in your calendar early in that day to remind yourself it is a discipline over-practice day.

Team Up with a "Mental" Coach

Many people perform better when they know someone is watching them or when they feel accountable to someone else. That's why many people need bosses or coaches to supervise them to success. A part of being mentally tough requires that you watch, evaluate, and are accountable to yourself. Yet sometimes, it can be quite helpful to conjure up a coach in your mind. This mental coach can inspire you, challenge you, and serve as a role model.

One of the first clients to whom I taught Gable discipline was Marianne, an information technology (IT) manager in an accounting firm. In the aftermath of a particularly challenging tax season, Marianne decided she needed to take a break from her career process goal of completing at least one course per semester toward her MBA. After a few weeks of rescheduling appointments with me, Marianne eventually came into my office and told me the following: "The last few weeks have been really tough. I had made up my mind to put school on hold, but then your story of Coach Gable got into my head. I began asking myself the question: What would Coach Gable expect?"

She went on to give other examples. When Marianne found herself procrastinating on finishing reports, she asked herself, "What would Coach Gable do if he had two reports to do and only 24 hours to complete them?" When Marianne found herself overwhelmed at the thought of finishing a tough homework assignment, she asked herself, "What would Coach Gable do if he needed help with his statistics homework?" And when Marianne put on a few pounds, she asked herself, "What would Coach Gable do if he needed to lose 10 pounds?" Asking the questions helped Marianne because she always assumed Coach Gable would do the right thing, whether it meant staying up late to complete both reports, meeting with the professor for help, or working out harder and watching her food intake to control her weight.

As Marianne continued to strive for success, she became more and more disciplined by asking again and again what her mental coach (Coach Gable) would do or expect in certain situations. Marianne was taking the easy way out less often than she had done earlier in her life. Her discipline was paying off: Marianne was actually becoming proud of herself. Her career was progressing, she was in better health, and she decided to stay on track with her MBA goal.

For the next several years, Marianne continued to use Coach Gable as her mental coach to increase her discipline and success. Marianne got to a point where whatever she set her mind to, she accomplished. With her MBA in hand, Marianne moved her way to the top of the corporate ladder and eventually started her own IT consulting business using Gable discipline to drive its success.

You can have more than one mental coach: one person may be more motivating to you in certain situations than in others. However, I don't suggest having more than two or three mental coaches to lean on, because you want your thought process to be clear and uncluttered. I have two mental coaches, both of whom happen to have been coaches in real life, and both of whom I have studied and met in person: Coach John Wooden and Coach Dan Gable. You may feel you know enough about either of these men to choose them as one of your mental coaches. Or you may select someone else. Choose someone whom you respect and who will push you to have the discipline needed for high-level success.

Write down the name of someone you will use as a mental coach.

My mental coach(es) will be: _____

Overdeliver

You've probably heard the phrase "underpromise and overdeliver." I find it quite common in business, and while I love the idea of overdelivering, I dislike very much the concept of underpromising. It's like turning your self-image thermostat down, or giving yourself an articulated excuse before you even begin a task. I prefer simply to focus on the overdelivering part. Overdelivering, or going above and beyond your promise of solid performance and service, requires unremitting discipline. Never underpromise on what you are indeed capable of delivering. Expect the absolute best of yourself, and if for some reason you find yourself falling short, become more disciplined by limiting temptation, over-practicing discipline, and invoking your mental coach.

I am certainly not suggesting that you set the bar higher on every task, every day; that approach would not represent focus. Instead, I am encouraging you to be optimistic by dreaming big. Don't ever be satisfied with less than your full potential. Go after your dreams by telling your employees, coworkers, bosses, and clients what you are capable of, and then use Gable discipline to live up to your word. Learn to become a get-it-done person. Don't make excuses, never give up, and watch your path to greatness begin to unfold before your very eyes.

Choose to Be Great

Mental Toughness Fundamental #10: Adopt Gable Discipline. *When you set your mind to do something, find a way to get it done . . . no matter what!*

Take the time to complete the following three tasks:

1. Write down the three components of Gable discipline (page 174), and set a phone reminder that says "Adopt Gable Discipline" for the first day of the month for the next 12 months.
2. Read 15 minutes from a book written by or about one of the most disciplined people you know about.
3. Choose one friend or coworker, and teach that person Gable discipline and the three ways to develop it.

Conclusion
The Minimum Requirements for Greatness

I have no doubt that you have the potential to achieve greatness: to be that professional who excels by constantly pushing the boundaries of leadership performance and making those around him or her better by being *the* positive role model of discipline and success. I know you can win more often in all parts of your life, and I can prove it.

Jot down your answer to the following two questions:

1. **What is one thing you have done well in the last 24 hours?** It doesn't have to be closing the biggest deal of your life. Just identify one success, big or small.

_____

2. **What is one thing you want to improve tomorrow?** Again, it doesn't have to be game-changing—just one small improvement is fine.

_____

By answering these two questions, you have just proved you have the potential for greatness. When I visited with him, Coach John Wooden told me that the greatest people in the world do two things well:

1. They give themselves credit where credit is due.
2. They relentlessly pursue improvement.

Nonetheless, greatness will not magically appear in your life without significant accountability, focus, and optimism on your part. Are you ready to commit fully to turning your potential into a leadership performance that will propel you to greatness? Are you ready to win? Tom Bartow, the executive coach profiled in Chapter 5, often addresses audiences with this catchphrase: "You are going to survive. So why not win?"

Now that you know what winning means to you, use your mental toughness fundamentals to start winning every day! The path to winning isn't blocked by insurmountable external barriers. It is blocked only by your hesitation to start or stick with the winning plan. If the mental toughness program were exceedingly complicated, time consuming, expensive, or scary, I could understand your hesitation. But it's not. Mirroring the way I summarize important takeaways at the end of a presentation or coaching session, I offer the following highlights of the three components and 10 mental toughness fundamentals of the *Executive Toughness* plan.

Start Winning by Knowing Who You Are and What You Want

Mental Toughness Fundamental #1: Define Your Win

Know your purpose and priorities to solidify your ability to win in the important aspects of life.

Mental Toughness Fundamental #2: Create Your Vision of Self-Image

Take 30 seconds every day to visualize who you want to be and how you want life to turn out, and dramatically increase the likelihood of achieving your win.

How in the world can you win the life you want without identifying your true purpose for being here, your greatest priorities in life, and how you want your life to turn out? Without knowing who you want to be and what you want to accomplish, you'll find it impossible to develop passion, motivation, and inspiration—the very bonding agents of accountability, focus, and optimism. Maxine Clark is living proof of the importance of knowing who you are and what you stand for.

Specific details elevate a vague life plan into a true vision of self-image that you can use to transform the way you think about yourself, your potential, and your future. Think about how motivational it must be for Steve to know who he wants to become and how he wants his life to be in five years. Anytime he finds himself off-track, he simply reviews his life purpose and priorities or replays his vision of self-image. Those simple actions reignite his fire for completing those tasks that are most important.

Start Winning with Accountability: Doing What *Needs* to Be Done

Mental Toughness Fundamental #3: Set Product Goals and Emphasize Process Goals

If you want to achieve greatness in life, you need to put significant emphasis on what it takes to get there.

Mental Toughness Fundamental #4: Prioritize the Priorities

If you want to achieve your product goals and live your vision of self-image, process goal completion must be the priority each and every day.

Mental Toughness Fundamental #5: Complete Daily Performance Evaluations

Take the time on a daily basis to evaluate your personal progress and effort, and you will inevitably learn to achieve your win.

Oftentimes, mental toughness catalyzes the transition from merely *wanting* to win to *actually* winning. The difference between the two is accountability and follow-through. Being accountable is a tremendous responsibility, a responsibility that will immediately allow you to perform at or above your potential more consistently.

Accountability also involves splitting your big product goals into daily process goals and scheduling time to complete them. Coach Wooden made clear the importance of accountability and self-evaluation.

Commit on a daily basis to using success logs and quarterly evaluations to track your progress and better control your success.

Start Winning with Focus: Improving Consistency and Execution

Mental Toughness Fundamental #6: Control Your Arousal State

Learn to control your arousal state and cause your confidence to build, your brain to function more effectively, and your successes to grow.

Mental Toughness Fundamental #7: Know Your Scripts

Develop your focus by knowing and practicing what you are going to say—before you say it!

Mental Toughness Fundamental #8: Prepare Mentally Every Day

Complete a 100-second mental workout every day to dramatically improve your focus and ability to execute consistently.

By understanding your ideal arousal state (IAS), maintaining basic physical fitness, and preparing yourself intellectually by knowing your markets, customers, and competitors, you become able to control your arousal state so that emotion doesn't get in the way of your focus.

Through accountability, you have defined the tasks that deserve your focus. Creating and memorizing scripts for key interactions helps you maintain focus. They build confidence and reduce the anxiety that often gets in the way of leadership performance.

All aspects of focus come together in the mental workout, one of the most effective methods known for training your body and mind to stay under control and perform to your potential. A centering breath settles you into your IAS; then you say your identity statement, run your vision of self-image and integrity highlight reel, and repeat the identity statement and centering breath. It is your training regimen to strengthen your focus like that of John Ertz who has successfully mastered the balance of personal and professional excellence.

Start Winning with Optimism: Overcoming All Obstacles

Mental Toughness Fundamental #9: Develop a Relentless Solution Focus

Within 60 seconds, replace all problem-focused thought with solution-focused thinking to dramatically improve your health, happiness, and success.

Becoming optimistic is one of the most critical pieces of your mental toughness puzzle because it means that you approach every situation with hope and confidence that you will succeed. Replace all negative thinking with relentless solution focus (RSF) within 60 seconds by using the RSF question, "What is one thing I can do differently to make this better?" When you answer that question instead of thinking about problems, you demonstrate your mental toughness and are well on your way to greatness.

Mental Toughness Fundamental #10: Adopt Gable Discipline

When you set your mind to do something, find a way to get it done . . . no matter what!

Along with dedication to results-driving Gable discipline, RSF is the surefire way to improve your confidence and control your outcomes like that of Jack Canfield so you become grounded in the rational optimism that drives happiness, health, success, and, ultimately, greatness.

Overcoming Obstacles

Certainly, achieving the success you want takes work. As you read in the stories I shared about my clients, you will have noticed that they often get stuck as they change their very approach to life. That's to be expected: if mental toughness were easy, everybody would succeed all of the time. Mental toughness is by definition abnormal and extraordinary. That's why it makes you different and results in your winning more often in all aspects of your life.

It is not only likely but also expected that you will face obstacles as you develop mental toughness. You may face tragedy or setbacks. You will fall down, your kids will get sick, your superiors will foolishly choose to overlook and disrespect you, and your competition inside or outside your firm will beat you from time to time. Part of mental toughness is understanding that the only true obstacles in life are self-imposed. You always have the choice to stay down or rise above. In truth, the only *real* obstacles to your ultimate success will come from within yourself and fall into one of the following three categories:

- **Apathy**, or the lack of passion
- **Laziness**, or the lack of motivation
- **Fear**, or the lack of confidence

Apathy

Oftentimes people show up in my office in what I call a "holding pattern." They are moving, but to nowhere in particular. It's quite common for people to think that if they just hang on long enough or keep themselves busy enough, they will end up at their desired destinations. Not true. Going with the flow and remaining in a holding pattern equates to a miserable and passionless life. You must decide where you want to go if you want to get anywhere in life. Don't allow yourself to get into a holding pattern while you try to figure out who you are or what you're supposed to do. Instead, decide who you *want* to be and what you *want* to do. If you are not sure what you are passionate about, use the following tips to help you find something important to reach for:

- Identify one thing you would really like to do with or in your life, and list the first three steps needed to make that a reality. Then schedule in your calendar when you will take action and complete the first step. For example, if you have always wanted to start your own e-business and you know the first step is securing funding to undertake market research, then go ahead and make an appointment with your banker to initiate a small business loan.
- Limit daily alcohol intake to absolutely no more than three drinks per day. Alcohol is a depressant, and more than a minimal use of alcohol quells passion and your quest for greatness.
- While doing cardio exercise, turn off the TV and headphones for 15 minutes and think about what you enjoy and what you could do differently to bring more passion into your life. Thinking while exercising opens your mind up to creativity and previously unthought-of options.

Laziness

Laziness is not a personality disorder! Laziness is a habit, and just like any other habit, it can be broken. Just as you learned to be lazy, you can teach yourself to be industrious. I have found that laziness breeds more laziness. When you start the day by sleeping past the alarm or cutting corners in the morning, you're more likely to continue that slothful attitude later in the day. Replace laziness with high productivity by following these two guidelines:

- **Sacrifice early, reward later:** When the alarm goes off, get up and get cranking on your daily to-do list. Only after you have checked off all of your daily need-to-get-completed tasks do you reward yourself by lying on the couch, turning on the TV, or browsing the Internet.

- **Visualize productiveness:** Use your mental workout to see into existence a more productive you. Highlight the key points such as getting up when the alarm goes off, completing tasks early in the day, maintaining energy in the middle of the day, and finishing the day strong by wrapping up on time. Be sure to include in your visualization the positive feeling that being productive causes.

Fear

You may experience a fear of failure to live up to your own goals and expectations. You may hold yourself back from giving your all in life because the thought of trying your hardest and still coming up short seems to be more painful than holding back a bit and always having an excuse such as, "If I had really wanted to, I could have accomplished anything. . . . I just never really wanted it."

Or you may live with the fear of failing to live up to others' expectations. "Good" boys and girls grow up always following directions and often become those who tend to need others' approval. They can become sought-after employees because they seek to impress and tend to be good at collaboration. Unfortunately, they often get off their own track when they feel compelled to please everyone else and answer to others' needs and desires. Some are so fearful of losing others' approval that they have no clue what they really want in life.

Either way you can learn to overcome your fear by doing the following:

- Learn to value your own opinions, needs, and wants just a bit more than you value others' opinions, needs, and wants. This doesn't give you permission to be self-righteous but rather will put you in a position to appreciate yourself while respecting others. It is incredibly healthy to value yourself, especially if you can do it while appreciating and listening to others.

- Decide on one important thing you want to accomplish and then go for it. Let it all hang out. Tell your friends about your goal, and then every day work with passion and energy. The truth is that when you let fear hold you back, you are guaranteed to fail. Giving your all will *dramatically* increase your chance for success. Build on your successes by continuing to take ownership of what *you* want, and watch your potential skyrocket.
- Learn to say no. You will have to learn to use the word *no*. You can't nor do you need to do everything. Focus on owning your feelings, and let others own theirs. Identify those tasks that cause your success and then commit to completing them. To do so, you need to say no to plenty of other requests. Will you disappoint others? Yes. But the alternative is chronically disappointing yourself.

The Minimum Requirements for Greatness

In addition to summarizing my main points at the end of a session or presentation, I ask my audience or client to do the same. Since this book is about what *you* need to do to become mentally tough, please take a moment to summarize your takeaways in terms of your three most important action items.

My top three action items for mental toughness are:

1. _____

2. _____

3. _____

By now, you will have noticed that I take channel capacity pretty seriously and I present ideas in sets of three. With that in mind, I can boil executive toughness down to the following top three action items, in order of importance:

1. **Complete your process goals every day . . . no excuses!** Assuming you have taken the time to develop your vision of self-image and product goals as well as the process goals needed to get there, completing the process goals every day will have an unbelievably powerful impact on your ability to perform at a leadership level and thereby achieve personal and professional greatness.
2. **Commit to replacing all negative or problem-focused thought with solution-focused thinking within 60 seconds (RSF).** Use RSF to once and for all train yourself to become optimistic, and watch not only your success but also your health and happiness increase significantly.
3. **Complete mental workouts and success logs five days per week.** Mental workouts and success logs will greatly enhance your ability to stay focused and accountable to process goal completion and RSF.

You can download a summary takeaway work sheet from my website at www.jasonselk.com. Take a moment to compare your takeaways with mine, and don't be surprised if we disagree. The takeaway comparison contributes to the greatness process because it represents the transmission of responsibility from me as the "teacher" to you as the individual who will do the work. The real value is realizing what is best for you.

In considering both your takeaways and mine, revise your takeaways to create the short list of your action items.

My revised top three action items to achieve the success I want in life are:

1. _____

2. _____

3. _____

Congratulate Yourself

Recognize that by taking time out of your busy life to read this book and complete the exercises, you have taken the first steps toward greatness. If you follow the *Executive Toughness* program or even just commit to your revised list of three action items, you will enhance your ability to achieve the success you want, increase your leadership performance, and become great. It won't be easy—greatness isn't supposed to be easy—but you can do it.

Choose to be great, *every day!*

Looking Forward

Once you commit to executive toughness, you'll wish all those around you had the same commitment to their own success. You may find that others lack direction, purpose, and focus. You may find that some colleagues bombard you day in and day out with problems and negative thinking. It may feel at times as if you are swimming against the current, because you are. Most people are indeed complacent, naively unaware of the greatness they could achieve.

It's your job to rise above the people who distract you from your purpose and goals.

Yet it's also likely that you'll find executive toughness to be contagious. Others will see your success and want to know your secret. You will become a role model for those around you. You will bring accountability, focus, and optimism to your team and become the key driver of achievement.

If you're the boss, you will find yourself introducing executive toughness concepts into the way you manage your people, because you will begin to expect accountability, focus, and optimism from those who work for you.

Organizations of all kinds have realized that when a critical mass of individuals commit to pursuing individual success through executive toughness, they together drive the achievement of collective objectives. Rarely is individual achievement a zero-sum game: when individuals win, the organization wins.

These organizations realize that executive toughness can be their solution to the problem of the scarcity of human ability throughout the modern business world. It provides a systematic and effective program that employees can grasp and, very important, find the time to incorporate into their daily lives.

When you see that executive toughness works for you, think about how you might introduce it to your colleagues, team, and organization. Choose one key person in your organization to introduce executive toughness to. Challenge him or her in turn to pass the knowledge on to one additional person. Quite soon, you'll witness the ripple effects of individual greatness and watch the overall success of your team or organization begin to soar.

Notes

Introduction

1. Chip and Dan Heath, *Switch: How to Change Things When Change Is Hard* (New York: Crown, 2010), 114.
2. Shane Murphy, *The Sport Psych Handbook* (Champaign, IL: Human Kinetics, 2005).

Chapter 1

1. Mark Scott, "The Bear Necessities," *Smart Business,* February 25, 2008, http://www.sbnonline.com/2008/02/the-bear-neces sities-how-maxine-clark-led-build-a-bear-to-success-by-creating-a-culture-stuffed-with-enthusiasm/?full=1&sectionid=corpor ate-culture-management-topics&edition=st-louis-editions.
2. Robin Sharma, *Discover Your Destiny* (New York: HarperCollins, 2005), 206.
3. Jim Collins, *Good to Great: Why Some Companies Make the Leap . . . and Others Don't* (New York: HarperCollins, 2001), 1.
4. James Collins and Jerry Porras, "Building Your Company's Vision," *Harvard Business Review* 74, no. 5 (1996): 65–77.

Chapter 2

1. Maxwell Maltz, *Psycho-Cybernetics: A New Way to Get More Living Out of Life* (New York: Pocket Books, 1989), 13.

Chapter 3

1. Troy Wilson and David Kohl, "Business Planning: A Roadmap for Success," *Agricultural Marketing,* 1997, http://agmarketing .extension.psu.edu/Business/WhtIsBusPlan.html.

2. James Collins and Jerry Porras, "Building Your Company's Vision," *Harvard Business Review* 74, no. 5 (1996): 65–77.

Chapter 4

1. Jim Loehr, *The Power of Full Engagement* (New York: Free Press, 2004), 3.
2. Stephen R. Covey, *First Things First* (London: Simon and Schuster, 1999), 38.
3. Brian Tracy, *Eat That Frog!* (San Francisco: Berrett-Koehler Publisher, 2001).

Chapter 5

1. Ben Hogan, *Ben Hogan's Five Lessons* (New York: Pocket Books, 1990), 113.

Chapter 6

1. John Medina, *Brain Rules* (Seattle: Pear Press, 2009).
2. Ibid.
3. Timothy Ferriss, *The 4-Hour Workweek* (New York: Crown, 2009).

Chapter 7

1. Ed Gruver, "The Lombardi Sweep," *The Coffin Corner* 19, no. 5 (1997): 3.

Chapter 8

1. Jack Nicklaus, *Golf My Way* (New York: Simon & Schuster, 2005), 79.
2. Shane Murphy, *The Sport Psych Handbook* (Champaign, IL: Human Kinetics, 2005).

Chapter 10

1. Nolan Zavoral, *A Season on the Mat* (New York: Simon & Schuster, 1998), 58.
2. Ibid.

Index

About the Author

Jason Selk, Ph.D., is the director of mental training for the St. Louis Cardinals and author of *10-Minute Toughness*. Jason is a regular contributor to ABC, CBS, ESPN, and NBC radio and television and has been featured in *Men's Health, Muscle and Fitness, Self, Shape, Stack,* and *Fitness* magazines. Jason utilizes his in-depth knowledge and experience of working with the world's finest business leaders, athletes, and coaches to help individuals and organizations develop the mental toughness needed for high level success. Jason's first book, *10-Minute Toughness*, is on-pace to be one of the bestselling sport psychology books of all time and Jason is considered one of the top performance coaches in the world.

Jason has experience providing services for the following clients: Anheuser-Busch, Blue Cross Blue Shield, Charles Schwab, Edward Jones, Enterprise Rent-A-Car, Northwestern Mutual, Wells Fargo, the National Collegiate Athletic Association (NCAA), Major League Baseball (MLB), the National Football League (NFL), the National Hockey League (NHL), USA Gymnastics, USA Skiing, USA Swimming, and many others.